# WATCHING UNTO PRAYER

*Four weeks of daily readings*

*from*

*Robert Murray M'Cheyne*

FREE PRESBYTERIAN PUBLICATIONS

Free Presbyterian Publications
133 Woodlands Road
Glasgow
G3 6LE


First published in *The Christian's Daily Companion* 1843

First published in this form 1988

Reprinted 1995


ISBN  0 902506 27 7


Typesetting by
Settle Graphics · Settle · North Yorkshire

Printing by
Craven Herald & Pioneer · Skipton · North Yorkshire

# Contents

# Foreword

EVEN 143 YEARS after his death, the name of Robert Murray McCheyne suggests to many the most ardent devotion to Christ's service, and vehement love for souls. He was not yet thirty when he died, and he had been a minister for only eight years; yet in that short time the Lord used him to an extent rarely seen. Just a year after his death, his friend, the Rev. Andrew Bonar, produced a book in his memory that has become a classic of its kind. In addition to an account of McCheyne's life, the *Memoir and Remains of Robert Murray McCheyne* contained many of his letters, twenty-eight sermons, and various other writings including poems. Two years later, another sizeable volume containing sixty-four sermons and fifteen lectures also found a large readership in those who treasured the memory of perhaps the saintliest minister of Christ they had ever known. By these books and their reprints, Robert McCheyne still speaks.

There is reason to think that the twenty-eight pieces of writing in the present publication are unknown to the general public. They were not sermons, but "Meditations and short practical comments on the most important doctrines and precepts of the Holy Scriptures". In 1843, the year that McCheyne died, a large volume titled, *The Christian's Daily Companion* was published for supplying morning and evening meditations on texts of Scripture, to aid the devotions of god-fearing people; and it was so designed as to cover the whole range of Christian doctrine. Its editor, the Rev. Dr. Paterson of Glasgow, obtained the help of thirty-one, well-known, evangelical ministers of the Church of Scotland. Between them they composed a book containing nearly 900,000 words whose first day's topics were "Creation" and "Communion with God", and those for the last day of the year were, "The Ransomed of the Lord" and "The Lamb for Ever and Ever".

Robert Murray McCheyne was apportioned the period, ninth to the twenty-second of April, and the following subjects: "The Second Coming of Christ"; "The Work of the Holy Spirit in Bringing Sinners to Christ and

Helping them Thereafter"; and "The Ministry of the Gospel". His handling of the texts which formed the basis of the meditations is all that might have been expected from such a gifted, wise and faithful expositor of the Word. As was his wont, the truth is expressed with a delightful simplicity and clarity. We commend this little book to everyone who is concerned to possess eternal life, and desires that, as was the case with Gaius, his soul may prosper.


Alexander McPherson
CONVENER, PUBLICATIONS COMMITTEE

September 1987

# 1. Lightning from the East

*For as the lightning cometh out of the east,*
*and shineth even unto the west; so shall also the coming of*
*the Son of man be.*

MATTHEW 24:27

WHAT A SOLEMN and glorious event is that spoken of in these words, the coming of the Son of man! His first coming was infinitely wonderful, when He left the bosom of His Father, emptied Himself of His glory, and Himself bare our sins on His own body on the tree. His second coming will be very different, but still infinitely wonderful. "Unto them that look for him shall he appear the second time, without sin, unto salvation" (Hebrews 9:28). May we be among the number of those who "love his appearing", who are "looking for that blessed hope", and who are "waiting for his Son from heaven, even Jesus, which delivered us from the wrath to come". Surely they have but cold love to Jesus that do not burn with desire to see the fair brow that was crowned with thorns.

1. Christ's coming will be terrible as lightning to His enemies. Nothing is more terrific than the lightning. It is so powerful, so sudden, so deadly in its stroke. The strongest man is like a straw before it. Much more terrible will Christ's appearing be to all unbelievers. To His own dear people it will be like the approach of summer. When they see the signs of His coming, they will say to one another, "the summer is nigh" (verse 32). "He shall come down like rain on the mown grass, as showers that water the earth" (Psalm 72:6). To poor waiting believers "He shall be as the light of the morning when the sun riseth, even a morning without clouds" (2 Samuel 23:4). To those that fear God's name in this dark world, "The Sun of righteousness shall rise with healing in his wings" (Malachi 4:2). The cry shall be one of ineffable joy to them, "Behold the Bridegroom cometh".

How different that day shall be to unconverted souls! "Woe unto you that desire the day of the Lord. To what end is it for you? The day of the Lord is darkness, and not light" (Amos 5:18). That day shall burn as an oven to you. "The Lord Jesus shall be revealed from heaven with his mighty angels, in flaming fire, taking vengeance on them that know not God, and that obey

1

not the gospel" (2 Thessalonians 1: 7-8). Then will be fulfilled that awful word, "All kindreds of the earth shall wail because of him" (Revelation 1:7), O! thou that obeyest not the gospel, where wilt thou hide from the lightning of His eye? Thou wilt say, Ah! there He is — the crucified One — whom I lightly esteemed. O! mountains and rocks fall on me and hide me from Him that sitteth on the throne, and from the wrath of the Lamb.

2. Christ's coming shall be sudden as lightning. What can be more awfully sudden than the lightning? A curtain of dark lowering clouds is hung over the sky. A death-like silence reigns over all nature. Not a leaf is stirred by the wind. When suddenly, "the voice of the Lord divideth the flames of fire". "The lightning cometh out of the east, and shineth even unto the west." And the loud pealing thunder shakes the wilderness. So shall the coming of the Son of man be. Whenever that glorious event shall take place, one thing is certain, that it shall be awfully sudden. A thief does not send word what hour he is coming to break up the house. "The day of the Lord so cometh as a thief in the night." It shall come "like travail on a woman with child". "As a snare shall it come on all them that dwell on the face of the whole earth." Many will be saying, I think the Saviour will not come at such and such a time. What says the word? "The Son of man cometh at an hour *when ye think not.*" Am I ready to meet him? Would it be a grief and terror to me, if what some Christians think were true, that Christ may come even now? Do I love His appearing? Do I obey that command, Song 3:11? Am I a wise or foolish virgin? Have I not only a lamp, and wick, and flame, but oil in the lamp? All these are infinitely momentous questions. Happy the soul that can answer, "Even so, come, Lord Jesus".

3. Christ's coming shall be conspicuous as lightning. Lightning cannot be hid. By all it is seen at the same moment. The labourer in the field, the artizan in the workshop, the servant at the mill — all see the flash; but in a far more perfect manner shall be the coming of the Son of man. "Behold he cometh with clouds; and every eye shall see him, and they also which pierced him." Jesus said to the high priest and all his accusers, "Hereafter shall *ye see* the Son of man sitting on the right hand of power, and coming in the clouds of heaven" (Matthew 26:64). And again it is written, "they shall look on him whom they pierced". O amazing truth! Those who will not look to Christ now must look then. Those who will not "behold the Lamb of God", to be saved by Him, must behold the Lamb coming in wrath to destroy them. O happy believer, you shall cry in that day, "This is our God, we have waited for him". "This is my Beloved, and this is my Friend." "My Lord and my God."

2

# 2.     Watching Unto Prayer

*But the end of all things is at hand:*
*be ye therefore sober, and watch unto prayer.*

1 PETER 4:7

1. OBSERVE where a believer stands. He stands within sight of the end of all things. He stands upon a watch-tower, high above the noise and the cares of this present evil world. Things temporal are beneath his feet, things eternal are spread out before him. This is the Bible description of a believer, "We look not at the things which are seen, but at the things which are not seen" (2 Corinthians 4:18). Consider how short the whole of a lifetime is. From the cradle to the grave is but a few steps. "The days of our years are threescore years and ten, and if by reason of strength they be fourscore years, yet is their strength labour and sorrow, for it is soon cut off, and we fly away." The half of men die before the age of twenty. Even when men lived many hundred years, it was but a span — a moment, compared to eternity. Methuselah lived 969 years, and he died. "My days are swifter than a weaver's shuttle. My days are swifter than a post. They are passed away as the swift ships. As the eagle hasteth to the prey."

The time of this world's continuance is short, "The end of all things is at hand". A little while, and the day of grace will be done. Preaching and praying will soon be over. The last sabbath sun will soon set. "My Spirit shall not always strive with men." Soon ministers will give over wrestling with the unbelieving world. A little while and the number of believers shall be complete. We shall come "unto a perfect man, unto the measure of the stature of the fulness of Christ". The parting cry of Christ was, "Surely I come quickly". Soon the sky shall open over our heads, and Christ shall come. A little while, and we shall stand before the great white throne. A little while, and the wicked shall not be. We shall see them going away into everlasting punishment. A little while, and the work of eternity shall be begun. We shall serve him day and night in His temple.

2. Observe the duties of a believer. "Be sober, and watch unto prayer." (i) *Be sober.* Let nothing dim the eye that is looking on eternal realities. Let nothing engross the heart that is already given away to Christ. Sit loose to

3

the dearest objects in this world. Brainerd mentions an instance of a poor Indian woman who, after her conversion, was resigned to the divine will in the most tender points. She was asked, "What if God should take away your husband from you, how do you think you could bear that?". She replied, "He belongs to God and not to me. He may do with him just as He pleases." An old divine says, "Build your nest upon no tree here; for you see God hath sold the forest to death, and every tree whereon we would rest is ready to be cut down, to the end we may flee, and mount up, and build upon the rock, and dwell in the holes of the rock".

Be sober in the griefs of this world. Weep as though you wept not. This world is the vale of tears. It is a Bochim. There are always some mourning. No sooner is the tear dried up on one cheek than it trickles down another. Still the believer should be sober and chastened in his grief. Weep not for those that died in the Lord; they are not lost, but gone before. The sun, when it sets, is not lost; it is gone to shine in another hemisphere. And so have they gone to "shine like the sun, in the kingdom of their Father". Weep not for those who died out of the Lord. When Aaron lost his two sons, "Aaron held his peace". Weep not over bodily pains and losses. Murmur not. Be sober. If you are in Christ, these are all the hell you will ever bear. When we win to the presence of Jesus, all our griefs shall look like children's griefs. A day in His banqueting house will make you "forget your poverty, and remember your misery no more".

Sit loose to this world's enjoyments. Be sober. In a little while you will be at your Father's table above, drinking the wine new with Christ, you will meet with all your brothers and sisters in the Lord, you will have pure joy in God through ceaseless ages. Do not be much taken with the joys that are here. If ever you are so much engrossed with any enjoyment here that it takes away your love for prayer, or for your Bible, or that it would frighten you to hear the cry, Behold the Bridegroom cometh — then your heart is *"overcharged"*. You are abusing this world.

(ii) *Watch*. "Knowing the time, that now it is high time to awake out of sleep, for now is our salvation nearer than when we believed." Nothing is more difficult than to watch. We are naturally like him who said, "a little more sleep, and a little more slumber, a little folding of the hands to sleep". One thing is essential to all true watching — the gift of the Holy Spirit. "Anoint thine eyes with eye-salve, that thou mayest see" (Revelation 3:18). Take out the beam that is in thine own eye. Not only abstain from dimming the spiritual eye, but clear it. What shall I watch? Watch the work of grace in thine own soul. Has God cast the seed into the field of thine heart? Then see if the blade appear, or the ear, or the full corn in the ear. Has your soul been made a vineyard of red wine? Then say often to your Beloved, "Let us get up early to the vineyards; let us see if the vine flourish, whether the tender grape appears, and the pomegranates bud forth" (Song 7:12). Watch thine enemies. You have enemies within, and enemies without. Many seek to take thy crown. "Cast all your care upon the Lord, for he careth for you. Be sober, be vigilant, for your adversary the devil, as a roaring lion, walketh about, seeking whom he may devour." Watch the Redeemer's cause. The disciples slept while Jesus' body sweated drops of blood. Many disciples do the same in our day. Lie not on a bed of ivory while Joseph is in affliction. Be one of the "watchmen over the walls of Jerusalem" (Isaiah 62). Be one of those who watch for the morning.

(iii) *Watch unto prayer.* Some watch and pray not. Right watching quickens prayer. Seest thou the wants, corruptions, infirmities, backslidings, temptations of thine own spirit, the heart deceitful above all things and desperately wicked, yea, unsearchably wicked to human eye. Watch unto prayer. Let the eye look within, and then above. Seest thou the cause of Jesus bleeding, Israel turning back before their enemies, plants of the Lord's planting withering, many walking no more with Jesus, Ephesus losing her first love, Laodicea turning lukewarm, ministers fainting in the day of adversity, Jonah fleeing from the presence of the Lord, the hands of Moses weary, Amalek prevailing against Israel? "Watch unto prayer."

Seest thou a spring-time of love, Immanuel coming over the mountains of Bether, winter departing, flowers appearing, showers of blessing falling? "Watch unto prayer." Soon Scotland's day of grace will be ended. "Ask ye of the Lord rain in the time of the latter rain." Hearest thou Ephraim bemoaning himself, the dry bones of Israel shaking, saints loving her stones? Pray for the peace of Jerusalem; never hold thy peace day nor night, give Him no rest — "Watch unto prayer."

# 3.    The Lord and His Rewards

*And, behold, I come quickly;*
*and my reward is with me, to give every man according*
*as his work shall be.*

REVELATION 22:12

THERE IS SOMETHING peculiarly sacred about a parting word.
When a father assembles his children round his dying bed, and gives them
his last affectionate counsels; you may be quite sure that as long as they have
hearts to feel they will remember and often ponder over his parting words.
Here are the parting words of the Lord Jesus. Here are the latest accents
that fell from the blessed lips of Immanuel. They fell on the ear of the
beloved John as he lay entranced on the shore of sea-girt Patmos, "Behold, I
come quickly".

1. *Observe the person who comes.* "Behold, I come." We may say, like the
disciples on the lake of Galilee, "It is the Lord". It is the First, and the Last,
and the living One, who was dead, and, behold, He is alive for evermore.
Jehovah-Jesus is the person who comes. He whose name is "Wonderful,
Counsellor, the mighty God, the everlasting Father, the Prince of peace".
He who is the image of the invisible God, by whom all things were created
that are in heaven, and that are in earth, visible and invisible.

It is Jesus that comes. He that walked on the sea of Galilee, sat wearied on
the well of Sychar, and wept beside the rocky sepulchre of Bethany. He that
was surety for sinners, who sweated blood in Gethsemane, who was silent
before Pilate, and who, through the eternal Spirit offered Himself without
spot to God on Calvary. "This same Jesus, which is taken up from you into
heaven, shall so come in like manner as ye have seen him go into heaven."

It is He who is the righteousness and strength of all His people. He who is
our life, He on whom we lean coming up from the wilderness, He who is
afflicted in all our afflictions; our tender Shepherd, our elder Brother; He
whom, having not seen, we love. It is He that comes. Surely every believer
will love His appearing. You may tremble who know not God, and obey not
the gospel. This is He whom you have lightly esteemed. He stood at your
door till His head was filled with dew, and His locks with the drops of the

night. You despised Him and neglected His great salvation. How will you bear to see Him coming in the clouds of heaven?

2. *Observe the time when He comes.* "I come quickly." Christians differ widely as to the time when Christ shall come. This diversity is not to be wondered at. "Of that day, and that hour, knoweth no man, no, not the angels which are in heaven, neither the Son, but the Father" (Mark 13:32). "Of the times and the seasons, brethren, ye have no need that I write unto you; for yourselves know perfectly that the day of the Lord so cometh as a thief in the night" (1 Thessalonians 5:1-2). Take it at the longest calculation, it will soon be here. He said, I come quickly, 1800 years ago. Much more now may we say, He comes quickly. A few days, and every eye shall see Him. The sun is waxing old — weary of shining on a Christ-despising world. The whole creation groans under the ever-increasing load of guilt and woe. The lines of prophecy are converging to a point. The cup of Popery is nearly full. The time, times, and half a time, are hastening to a close. The souls below the altar are crying with a loud voice, "How long, O Lord". The Euphrates is drying up, that the way of the kings of the East may be prepared. There is a noise and a shaking among the dry bones of Israel. "In a moment, in the twinkling of an eye" the once crucified, now exalted, but long-despised Jesus shall come. "Unto them that look for him shall he appear the second time, without sin, unto salvation." Oh! believer, let this solemn truth make thee patient under the frown and contumely of an unbelieving world. Hold thy possessions with a slack hand. "Take heed, lest at any time your heart be overcharged with surfeiting, and drunkenness, and cares of this life, and so that day come upon you unawares." Behold, I come quickly!

3. *Observe what He brings with Him.* "My reward is with me." Christ Himself shall be the greatest reward of His people. "Fear not, Abram, I am thy shield and thy exceeding great reward." Any place would be heaven if we were with Christ. No place would be heaven without Him. "Whom have I in heaven but thee?" Oh to talk with Him as Moses and Elijah did on the mount of transfiguration, to hear Him speak gracious words, to lean our head where John leaned his, to hold Him, and not to let Him go, to behold that countenance which is as Lebanon, excellent as the cedars, to have Him turning upon us His eyes of divine tenderness and holy love — that will be a reward.

He has many crowns of righteousness to give to them that love His appearing. He has "the harps of God". He has "authority over ten cities" to give to His own. He has a kingdom prepared for them before the foundation of the world. He has a place beside Him on His throne. But He Himself will be our greatest reward, "I will give him the morning star".

4. *Observe what He will do.* He will give every man according as his work shall be. Christ is to be Judge of all. "For the Father judgeth no man, but hath committed all judgment unto the Son" (John 5:22). This is part of Christ's reward, that every knee shall bow to Him. It is fitting that He that stood silent before the Jews, and at the bar of Pilate, and was buffeted, spit upon, and condemned, should sit on the throne and judge His enemies. It will be greatly to the joy of Christ's people in that awful day, when they receive their reward from the hand that was pierced for them. It will make all unbelievers stand speechless when He to whom they have always said, Depart from us, shall say to them, Depart from me, ye cursed. Oh! that we may obtain mercy of the Lord in that day.

> "See the Judge *our* nature wearing,
> Clothed in majesty divine;
> You who long for His appearing,
> Then shall say, This God is mine;
> Gracious Saviour, own me in that day for thine."

# 4.    A Right to the Tree of Life

*Blessed are they that do his commandments,*
*that they may have right to the tree of life, and may enter in*
*through the gates into the city.*
REVELATION 22:14

1. *LET US MEDITATE on the character of the saved.* "They that do his commandments." All that are on the road to heaven, are not only a justified people, but a sanctified people. This was God's end in choosing us. "Whom

he did foreknow, he also did predestinate to be conformed to the image of his Son." If any man be chosen to salvation, it is through sanctification of the Spirit. He has chosen us in Christ before the foundation of the world, that we should be holy. This was Christ's great end in dying for us, that He might make us a holy nation. "Christ loved the church, and gave himself for it, that he might sanctify and cleanse it by the washing of water through the word." He laid down the unspeakable price for this. He became a man, He became a curse for this. He groaned, sweated blood, was bruised, bowed His head, gave up the ghost for this; that He might have liberty to make us free, humble, self-denied, loving, pure as He Himself is pure. This is the Holy Spirit's end in dealing with us. It would not be righteous in Him to dwell in an unjustified soul. It is no rest for the dove of heaven. He therefore awakens the soul — discovers to the man his guilt, depravity, lothesomeness. He glorifies Christ in the man's soul — destroys the face of the covering that is over the carnal heart. He softens the rocky heart, and inclines and engages the will to cleave to the Lord Jesus Christ alone for righteousness. Then He sees no iniquity in that man. He says of that soul, This is my rest; here will I dwell, for I have desired it. He writes all the law in that heart, Jeremiah 31:33. He does not omit one of the commandments. The man cries out, "I delight in the law of God after the inward man" (Romans 7:22). And not only does He give him the will, but the ability, to serve God; "It is God that worketh in you both to will and to do of his good pleasure" (Philippians 2:13).

O my soul, art thou one of those that do His commandments? Have I come into the bonds of the new covenant, and got the law put in my inward parts, and written on my heart? Does Christ stretch forth His hand to me, saying "Behold, my mother and my brethren. For whosoever shall do the will of my Father, the same is my brother, and sister, and mother" (Matthew 12:50). On this my eternity hangs. If I receive an unholy gospel I shall perish. They are ungodly men who "turn the grace of God into lasciviousness". The branches that bear no fruit He taketh away. They that are saved are they that do His commandments.

2. *Let us meditate on the blessedness of the saved.* "Blessed are they that do his commandments, that they may have right to the tree of life, and may enter in through the gates into the city." Holiness is its own reward. To be holy is to be happy. God is happy because He is infinitely holy. The devil never can be happy because he has lost every spark of holiness. The first rest of the believing soul is when he comes to Christ and finds pardon. But there is a further and sweeter rest when he learns of Christ, who is meek and

lowly in heart, Matthew 11:28-29. Holiness is the river of God's pleasure, and therefore it fills the soul that drinks of it with divine joy. But it has a further reward.

(i) *They have right to the tree of life.* Adam lost us that right when he fell. "God drove out the man: and he placed at the east of the garden of Eden cherubims, and a flaming sword which turned every way, to keep the way of the tree of life." In vain did Adam strive to find a secret entrance. Perhaps he tried to creep through the embowering thickets, or through some wooded pass. Perhaps he tried to enter under cloud of midnight, or by morning's early dawn, before the birds began their matin praise. But all in vain; that flaming sword "turned every way, to keep the way of the tree of life". Adam's children, up to this day, have spent their strength and ingenuity in the same vain attempt. They have gone about to establish their own righteousness. But all have found — a few on this side of eternity, and some, by fearful experience, on the other side — that the flaming sword of divine justice still turns every way, to keep the way of the tree of life. No — not every way. There is "a new and living way, which he hath consecrated for us through the vail, that is to say, his flesh". A second Adam came, the Lord from heaven. He gave Himself to the flaming sword of justice. A voice was heard, "Awake, O sword, against my Shepherd, and against the man that is my fellow, saith the Lord of hosts". And now that slain Lamb of God says, "I am the way; no man cometh unto the Father but by me". The guiltiest may enter in by Jesus. And hear how sweetly He says, "To him that overcometh will I give to eat of the tree of life, which is in the midst of the paradise of God" (Revelation 2:7).

O my soul, like Ephesus thou hast left thy first love, yet this promise is to thee. In Jesus thou hast *a right* to the tree of life. "He is faithful and just to forgive us our sins, and to cleanse us from all unrighteousness." I that in myself have a right to a place in hell, in Christ have a right to a place under the shadow of the tree of life in the midst of the paradise of God.

(ii) *May enter in through the gates into the city.* Here we are on our way to the heavenly city. We are coming up from the wilderness. Sometimes we have clouds between us and Christ — doubts as to our conversion — our union to Christ — our new nature. There all clouds and doubts shall flee away. Here we have diverse temptations from indwelling sin, from the world, from our adversary the devil; there temptations cannot come. Here we have no city where the most are righteous. We can hardly speak the name of Jesus in the streets, but we are made the song of the drunkard. There the inhabitants are all righteous — "there shall in no wise enter into it any thing that defileth". None but the holy angels, and the brothers and sisters of Christ shall be there. The song of eternity shall be, Worthy is the Lamb. Here we love Christ unseen. Often He withdraws Himself and is gone. We seek Him and find Him not. There we shall be for ever with the Lord. We shall see Him as He is. We shall be with Him, and behold His glory which His Father gave Him. We shall say without another doubt to all eternity, "I am my Beloved's, and his desire is toward me". This is the reward of the sanctified. O my soul, is this reward for thee? Welcome light afflictions, which are but for a moment. Welcome sweet cross, that I must bear for Jesus. Roll round, swift years. Hasten the day of His espousals — the day of the gladness of His heart and mine, that I may enter with all His redeemed through the gates that are all praise.

# 5.     Plenteous Redemption

*Let Israel hope in the Lord:*
*for with the Lord there is mercy, and with him is plenteous redemption.*
*And he shall redeem Israel from all his iniquities.*

PSALM 130:7-8

IN THESE WORDS we have a believing Israelite inviting all his people to come to the same Fountain where he has found pardon and peace with God. He had been himself awakened by the Holy Spirit to feel the awful "depths" of sin and misery in which he was sunk by nature, and by practice. On his knees, beneath the heart-searching eye of God, he felt that he was "under sin", that his "mouth must be stopped", and that he could not be just with God" (verse 3). "If thou, Lord, shouldest mark iniquities, O Lord, who shall stand?" But even in these depths the free mercy of God was reached forth to him; the scales were made to fall from his eyes by the eyesalve of the Spirit,

11

and the glorious discovery was made to his soul, that there is a way of forgiveness open to the vilest of men, verse 4. "But there is forgiveness with thee, that thou mayest be feared." With intensest anxiety did this believing soul now wait for the Lord. Those only who have experienced the dawning of the Sun of righteousness on their own soul, can know what it is to "wait for the Lord more than they that watch for the morning". More anxiously than the sick man on his bed, "full of tossings to and fro", longs for the first gleam of morning light coming in at his window; more anxiously than the weary Levite, keeping watch upon the temple wall, turned his eye toward the east, to see if the day began to break over mount Olivet; more anxiously far did this believing soul now wait for fuller discoveries of the fair face of Immanuel, and for a richer experience of the power of Jesus to purge the conscience, and purify the heart.

But no man can be contented to go to the Well of salvation alone. Joy in Christ is not a selfish joy. A man may have gold without wishing others to share with him. A man may have earthly learning, and be proud to keep it to himself. But the moment a man has found Christ, his cry is, "Come, see a man which told me all things that ever I did". O! that all I love but knew Him. "Let Israel hope in the Lord, for with the Lord there is mercy, and with him is plenteous redemption, and he shall redeem Israel from all his iniquities."

O sinner, whoever thou art, here are three amazing reasons why thou shouldest hope in the Lord. Satan would drive thee to despair, as if there was no hope that such an one as thou art could be saved. But as God is true, here is a door of hope for thy perishing soul.

1. *"With the Lord there is mercy."* God is such a God that with Him there is mercy. Mercy dwells in Him as in a fountain. All the mercy that is in the universe flows from Him. Mercy is compassion to those who deserve no compassion, but infinite wrath. It was mercy that made God spare fallen man, and not cast the world speedily into hell. It was mercy that made Him give His only begotten Son. It was mercy that made Him choose, awaken, and draw any sinner to Christ. He never saved any but out of free sovereign mercy. There is none so vile but God can save him without prejudice to His justice, truth, holiness, or majesty. God has saved as vile wretches, in time past, as any vile wretches that need now to be saved. Manasseh, once a monster in human form, is now a white-robed saint before the throne. The dying thief is this day with Christ in paradise. The murderers of Jesus are now tuning their harps of gold, and singing, "Worthy is the Lamb".

12

This is good news for thee, O vilest of men — for thee who has sinned against light and against convictions. I do not know that God will save thee, but I know that if He does, it will be in perfect accordance with His nature. "He delighteth in mercy."

2. *With Him is plenteous redemption.* When the manna fell upon the face of the wilderness round the camp of Israel, there was a plentiful supply for the many thousands of Israel. "He that gathered much had nothing over, and he that gathered little had no lack." So it is with Christ. He is freely offered to every creature. We are not straitened in Christ, but in our own hearts. "With him is plenteous redemption." No sinner ever came to Christ, and found the Fountain of forgiveness dried up. One of the texts that was instrumental in the conversion of John Bunyan was this, "Yet there is room" (Luke 14:22). Undone sinner, let this text lead thee to Christ. Many have come to Christ since the days of Abel. Thousands have entered through the strait gate, and are now His believing people on earth, or His glorified people in heaven. "But yet there is room." There is room for thee under Christ's wings. "With him is plenteous redemption." Brainerd once asked one of his converted Indians, "Do you see enough in Christ for the greatest of sinners?" She replied, "O enough, enough, for all the sinners in the world, if they would but come". And when he asked her if she would not tell others of the goodness of Christ; turning herself about to some poor Christless souls who stood by, she said, "O there is enough in Christ for you, if you would but come. O strive, strive to give up your hearts to him." Sinner, let the words of this poor believing Indian sink into thy heart. There is enough in Christ for thee, for with Him is plenteous redemption. O! take up the words of the returning prodigal, "How many hired servants of my father's have bread enough, and to spare, and I perish with hunger; I will arise and go to my father".

3. *He redeems from all iniquities.* If you drop a pebble into the bosom of the ocean, it is covered out of sight in a moment. But if you were to carry an immense rock and plunge it into the same ocean, it would be equally covered. So is it with the least of sinners, and the chief of sinners, when they come to Christ. There is no difference. The ocean of the blood of Jesus covers both equally. All sinners that come to Christ are equally justified in the sight of God. He will redeem Israel from all his iniquities. Christ is no half-saviour. His work is perfect. Dost thou believe in Christ? Then "all the transgressions that thou hast committed shall not be mentioned unto thee". Canst thou say the sweetest words that human lips ever uttered, "My

13

Beloved is mine?" Then on the authority of Him who cannot lie, I say to thee, "As far as east is from the west, so far hath he removed thy transgressions from thee". But perhaps thou sayest, However far removed, God's all-seeing eye may still be fixed on them. This cannot be; for thou canst say with Hezekiah, "Thou hast cast all my sins behind thy back". Nay, they are not only behind God's back, but out of sight, for it is written, "Thou wilt cast all their sins into the depths of the sea". But are they not to be found in God's book of remembrance? Listen to His own gracious declaration, "I have blotted out as a thick cloud thy transgressions, and as a cloud thy sins". But God can remember my sins, even though He has blotted them out of His book. Here again His own word, "I will forgive their iniquity, and I will remember their sin no more". But surely if God were to search out my sins He would find them somewhere, and condemn me in the judgment. Fear not, O troubled soul, this cannot be; for it is written, "The iniquity of Israel shall be sought for, and there shall be none; and the sins of Judah, and they shall not be found".

# 6. · Bought with a Price

*For ye are bought with a price: therefore glorify God in your body, and in your spirit, which are God's.*

1 CORINTHIANS 6:20

IN THESE WORDS we have the history of a believer.

1. *There was a time when he did not belong to God.* This is implied when it is said, "ye are bought with a price"; for a man does not buy what is already his own. An unconverted soul does not belong to God. In one sense, indeed, all things belong to God; for "the earth is the Lord's, and the fulness thereof". He says, "Every beast of the forest is mine, and the cattle upon a thousand hills". And again, "the Lord hath made all things for himself, yea,

14

even the wicked for the day of evil". Still, it is also true that the wicked do not belong to God. They are not His portion, His inheritance, His purchased possession. They are lost. They are sold under sin. When a fisherman draws his nets, and finds a great many bad fish among the good ones, he does not count the bad ones as his own. He gathers the good into vessels, and casts the bad away. So does God look upon lost souls. He says to them, "Ye are not my people, and I will not be your God".

God does not reign in unconverted souls. It is true He reigns over them, as He does over the wild beasts of the forest, and over the wild waves of the sea. He makes their wrath to praise Him. He holds them in with bit and bridle. But God does not reign in their hearts. The devil reigns there, and not God. "The heart of an unconverted man is the devil's house" (Mark 3:27).

O! it is good for me to look unto the rock whence I was hewn, and to the hole of the pit whence I was digged. Truly I can say, like Hezekiah, "Thou hast loved my soul from the pit of corruption". Should I not add, "I shall go softly all my years in the bitterness of my soul?".

2. *The happy change.* "Ye are bought with a price." When a man has bought anything, and paid for it, more especially if it has cost him a great price, he says, "This is mine". So it is with God and the believer. He has laid down a price for him, the pearl of great price. And now He says of every believing soul, "Fear not, for I have redeemed thee, I have called thee by thy name, thou art mine". The moment that Jesus spreads His skirt over a poor dying polluted sinner, the voice of the Father is heard saying, "Deliver him from going down to the pit: I have found a ransom". There never was a possession so completely belonging to any one as a redeemed soul belongs to God. We are His by creation, "He hath made us, and not we ourselves". We are His by preservation. "In him we live, and move, and have our being." How many years He preserved us when we were cutting at the hand that kept us out of hell. We are His by election. "Ye have not chosen me, but I have chosen you." "Fear not, O Jacob, my servant, and thou Jeshurun whom I have chosen." We are His by redemption. "I lay down my life for the sheep." "This is my body broken for you." We are His by the indwelling Spirit. "I will dwell in them and walk in them, and I will be their God, and they shall be my people." Accordingly, we are peculiarly dear to God. "Since thou wast precious in my sight, thou hast been honourable, and I have loved thee." God puts more value upon one believer than upon all the ungodly in the world. He is very kind to the ungodly; he gives them food and

15

raiment; houses and riches, health and pleasures, sunshine and showers; and yet He gives a child of God more in one day than He gives to all the ungodly during their whole existence. He gives His own children — forgiveness, peace with God, and the Holy Spirit. Truly we are not our own, we are bought with a price.

3. *The blessed duty flowing from this.* "Wherefore glorify God," etc. This duty is simply the resignation of soul and body into His hands, for time and for eternity. Take an example in one of the holiest and most eminent divines that ever lived. "I have been before God, and have given myself, all that I am, and have, to God; so that I am not, in any respect, my own. I can challenge no right in this understanding, this will, these affections which are in me. Neither have I any right to this body, or any of its members — no right to this tongue, these hands, these feet; no right to these senses, these eyes, these ears, this smell, or this taste; I have given myself clean away, and have not retained anything as my own. I gave myself to God in my baptism, and I have been this morning to Him, and told Him that I gave myself *wholly* to Him" (President Edwards). Or take the example of a dear boy who died about eight years old, and who was evidently taught by the same Spirit. One evening, near his death, he said to his watchful mother, "Mother, I think I belong to Him". She asked, "To whom, my child?". He replied, "To God, mother; my will, my understanding, my affections; I am God's boy altogether, mother".

O my soul, dost thou know anything of this? Canst thou say, "I am my Beloved's, and his desire is toward me?" Is it the chief desire of my heart to glorify God by fleeing from all sin? When the world comes and says, Come with us, stolen waters are sweet; my soul replies, Sinful world, I am not yours, I am the Lord's. When Satan says, Come with me, thou shalt not surely die; my soul cries out, Get thee behind me, Satan, I am not yours. I was once yours, but now I am bought with a price; I am Christ's. When sin within me says, Come and taste a little worldly pleasure; my heart replies, I am not thine — I am not my own, I am bought with a price — therefore will I glorify God in my body and my spirit, which are His.

# 7.  Christ Despised and Rejected

*He came unto his own, and his own received him not.*
JOHN 1:11

IN THIS CHAPTER John describes the coming of the Son of God into the world, and His rejection by those whom He came to save, in three different ways. In verse 5 he says, "The light shineth in darkness, and the darkness comprehended it not". When Jesus came to this world, it was like the rising of "the bright and morning star"; but the hearts of men were covered over with murky vapours, like those that settled over Egypt in that night when the "darkness might be felt", so that the heavenly radiance of Immanuel was not allowed to shine upon their souls. To those that knew Him He was "the light of men", "the morning Star", "the Sun of righteousness", the "morning without clouds"; but all the rest of the world comprehended it not.

Is it not still the same? "We know that we are of God, and the whole world lieth in wickedness." On many souls Christ has arisen with healing in His wings, so that we can say to them, "Arise; shine, for thy light is come, and the glory of the Lord has risen upon thee". But, ah! the most have never admitted the sweet, soft, peace-bringing beams of Jesus to shine into their dark hearts. "The God of this world hath blinded the minds of them that believe not, lest the light of the glorious gospel of Christ, who is the image of God, should shine into them." They know not whither they are going. Their feet are ready to stumble on the dark mountains. "The path of the wicked is as darkness; they know not at what they shall stumble".

Again, in verse 10, it is written, "He was in the world, and the world was made by him, and the world knew him not". Strange visit to this fallen world! He who "hung the earth upon nothing" — He who said, "Let there be light, and there was light" — He who "formed man of the dust of the ground, and breathed into his nostrils the breath of life" — He "by whom were all things created that are in heaven, and that are on earth" — that glorious being came to His own world, "God manifest in the flesh". Surely all his creatures will run to worship and adore Him. Surely they will "worship and bow down; they will kneel before the Lord their maker". Not so: "the world knew him not". They knew Him not at His birth. He left the

17

hallelujahs of the heavenly world for the manger at Bethlehem. A few shepherds from the fields of Bethlehem came and kneeled to Him; and the wise men saw and adored the infant King; but the most despised Him. "He is despised and rejected of men." "She wrapped him in swaddling-clothes, and laid him in a manger, for there was no room for them in the inn." They knew Him not during His life. Few believed on Him. They called Him glutton, wine-bibber, deceiver. Once they sought to cast Him over the rocks. Often they plotted to kill Him. He that had all things now wanted every thing. "Certain women ministered to him of their substance" (Luke 8:3). He had no money to pay His tribute. The creatures of His hand had a warmer bed than He. "The foxes have holes, the birds of the air have nests, but the Son of man hath not where to lay his head." "Every man went to his own home; Jesus went to the mount of Olives." Another time He sat wearied on a well, and said to a poor woman, "Give me to drink". He that was God over all, blessed for ever, could say, "I am a worm and no man". The world know Him not to this hour. The offence of the cross has not ceased. The way of salvation by Christ for us is still despised by most. He who is a sanctuary to all them that believe, is a stumbling-stone and rock of offence to most. O my soul, canst thou believe on Jesus when the world despise Him? Canst thou be one of the little flock? Canst thou enter in at "the strait gate, and walk on the narrow way", with an unbelieving world on every side?

Again, in verse 11 it is written, "He came unto his own, and his own received him not". In John 19:27, the same words are rendered more fully, *"to his own home"*. To see the full meaning of the passage before us, we must adopt the same reading here: "He came unto his own home, and his own family received him not."

The Jews were, as it were, His own family; and when He came to them, it was like coming to His own home. It was He who called their father Abraham, and separated them from among the nations to be a peculiar treasure: "He said, Surely they are my people, children that will not lie: so he was their Saviour. In all their affliction he was afflicted, and the angel of his presence saved them: in his love and in his pity he redeemed them; and he bare them, and carried them all the days of old" (Isaiah 63:8-9). He was the substance of all their types. He was the true pillar-cloud that guided their fathers, the true bread from heaven; He was the rock that followed them. He was the true Isaac the child of promise, the prophet like unto Moses, the David the beloved, the true Solomon the prince of peace. Though to all the

18

world He may appear "without form or comeliness, having no beauty that they should desire him"; yet surely His own Israel will receive Him as "the rose of Sharon and the lily of the valleys". Ah no! *He came unto his own, and his own received him not*. They cried, "Not this man, but Barabbas". "Away with him, away with him, crucify him, crucify him." "His blood be upon us, and upon our children." The rulers derided Him. The very thieves railed at Him. They shoot out the lip, they wag the head, they give Him vinegar to drink.

To this day His own receive Him not. Ah! think, sinner, whom it is you are despising. Did you ever see the son of a king lay by his robes and his glory, become a poor man, and die in misery, and all for nothing? Do you think the Lord Jesus Christ left His Father's love and the adoration of angels, and became a worm and died under wrath, and all for no purpose? Is there no wrath lying upon your soul? Have you no need of such a Saviour? Why then do you delay to flee to Him?

# 8.    Inability to Come to Christ

*No man can come to me,*
*except the Father, which hath sent me, draw him: and I will*
*raise him up at the last day.*
JOHN 6:44

1. *HOW AMAZING is the depravity of the natural heart!* The scriptures abundantly teach us this. All faithful ministers lift up their voice like a trumpet to show the people this; and it is the first work of the Holy Spirit on the heart to convince of sin. There is not in the Word of God a more fearful discovery of the depravity of the natural heart than in these words. David says, "Behold, I was shapen in iniquity, and in sin did my mother conceive me" (Psalm 51:5). God says by the prophet Isaiah, "I knew that thou

19

wouldest deal very treacherously, and wast called a transgressor from the womb" (Isaiah 48:8). And Paul says, "We were by nature the children of wrath, even as others" (Ephesians 2:3). But here we are told that the impotency of a natural man, and his aversion from Christ, are so great that they cannot be overcome by any power less than divine. "No man can come unto me, except the Father, which hath sent me, draw him." There never was a teacher like Christ. "Never man spake like this man." He spoke with such authority, not like the scribes, but with a heavenly dignity and power. He spoke with such wisdom; He spoke the truth without any imperfection; His teaching was pure light from the Fountain of light. He spoke with such love, with the love of One who was to lay down His life for His hearers. He spoke with such meekness, bearing the contradiction of sinners against Himself, when reviled, reviling not again. He spoke with such holiness, for it was "God manifest in the flesh". And yet all this did not draw them. There never was a more precious gift laid at the feet of sinners. "My Father giveth you the true bread from heaven. I am the bread of life. He that cometh to me shall never hunger, and he that believeth on me shall never thirst." The very Saviour their perishing souls needed was now before them. His hands were stretched out to them. He was within their reach. He offered Himself to them. Yet they would not come to Him. Oh! the desperate blindness, hardness, deadness, and wickedness of the unconverted heart. Nothing but Almighty grace can change it. Oh! graceless man, your friends warn you, your ministers cry aloud to you, the whole Bible pleads with you; Christ, with all His benefits, is set before you; and yet, unless the Holy Spirit be poured upon your heart, you will remain an enemy of the cross of Christ, and the destroyer of your own soul. "No man can come unto me, except the Father, which hath sent me, draw him."

2. *How invincible is the grace of Jehovah!* No creature power can draw the sinner to Christ. Demonstrations, miraculous evidence, threatening, invitation, may all be used in vain. Jehovah alone can draw the soul to Christ. He pours out His Spirit with the word, and the soul is sweetly and powerfully inclined to run to Jesus. "Thy people shall be willing in the day of thy power." "Is any thing too hard for the Lord?" "The king's heart is in the hand of the Lord, as the rivers of water; he turneth it whithersoever he will." Take an example: A Jew was sitting at the receipt of custom, near the gate of Capernaum. His brow was furrowed with the marks of covetousness, and his jealous eye exhibited all the low cunning of the publican. Very probably he had heard much of Jesus; perhaps he had heard Him preach by the shore

of the lake of Galilee; still his worldly heart was unchanged, for he remained at his wicked trade, sitting by the receipt of custom. The Saviour passed that way, and as He bent His eyes upon the busy Levi, said, "Follow me". He said no more. He used no argument, no threatening, no promise. But the God of all grace breathed on the publican's heart, and he was made willing; "he arose and followed him". It pleased God, who worketh all things according to the counsel of His own will, to give Matthew a saving glimpse of the excellency of Jesus; a drop fell from heaven upon his heart, and melted it; he smelled the sweet savour of the Rose of Sharon. What is all the world to Matthew now? He cares not for its gains, its pleasures, its praises, any more. In Christ he sees what is sweeter and better than them all. He arose and followed Jesus.

Let us learn that a simple word may be blessed to the saving of precious souls. Often we are tempted to think there must be some deep and logical argument to bring men to Christ. Often we put confidence in high-sounding words. Whereas it is the simple exhibition of Christ carried home by the Spirit, which awakens, enlightens, and saves. "Not by might, nor by power, but by my Spirit, saith the Lord of hosts." If the Spirit be breathing on the people, these little words, "Follow Jesus", spoken in love, may be blessed to the saving of a whole congregation.

Let us learn to give the whole praise and glory of our salvation to the free, sovereign, efficacious grace of Jehovah. An old divine says, "God was so angry with Herod for not giving Him the glory of his eloquence, that the angel of the Lord smote him immediately, and he died a miserable death; he was eaten of worms, and gave up the ghost. But if it be very sinful in a man to take to himself the glory of such a qualification as eloquence, how much more a man's taking to himself the glory of divine grace, God's own image, and that which is infinitely God's most excellent, precious, and glorious gift?" How many times, in the first chapter of Ephesians, does Paul insist upon it that we are saved by free, unmerited grace? And how fully does John ascribe the whole glory of salvation to the free grace of the Lord Jesus? "Unto him that loved us, and washed us from our sins in his own blood, and hath made us kings and priests unto God and his Father, to him be glory and dominion for ever. Amen." How solemn are the words of President Edwards, in his Personal Narrative! "The doctrines of God's absolute sovereignty and free grace, in showing mercy to whom He would show mercy; and man's absolute dependence on the operations of the Holy Spirit, have very often appeared to me as sweet and glorious doctrines. These doctrines have been much my delight. God's sovereignty has ever appeared to me a great part of His glory. It has often been my delight to approach God and adore Him as a sovereign God, and ask sovereign mercy of Him."

> "O! to grace how great a debtor
> Daily I'm constrained to be!
> Let that grace, Lord, like a fetter,
> Bind my wandering heart to thee."

# 9. Spirit of Truth the Only Guide to Truth

*Howbeit when he, the Spirit of truth, is come, he will guide you into all truth: for he shall not speak of himself; but whatsoever he shall hear, that shall he speak: and he will shew you things to come.*

JOHN 16:13

1. *LET US MEDITATE on the glorious person here spoken of.* "The Spirit of truth." A little before Jesus had called Him "another Comforter", and "the Comforter", because He is the Author of all true divine comfort in the soul of man. He alone pierces the heart with deep conviction of sin, and binds up the broken-hearted by healing discoveries of Christ. "These words" — the Comforter — (says an eminent Christian) "seem immensely great, enough to fill heaven and earth." But here He is called "the Spirit of truth"; for two reasons: (i) Because He sees all things truly. He is the omniscient One. He sees sin as it is, in all its infinite blackness. He sees the heart of man as it is; His eye penetrates to the deepest recesses of the ungodly heart. He sees Christ as He is, in all His infinite excellency and glory. "He searches all things, yea, the deep things of God" (1 Corinthians 2:10). He sees the gospel

22

in all its divine wisdom and pure heavenly grace. (ii) Because He teaches all things truly. He is the Fountain of life and light to the soul of man. When He comes to the soul, He quickens and enlightens in the same moment. He reveals the truth, as it is in Jesus, without any imperfection, without any cloud or error. If there be any dimness in our view of divine things, the fault does not lie in the Teacher, but in the perverse heart of the disciple. He does His part with divine perfection, revealing the Mediator in all His matchless beauty, fulness, and grace. Earthly teachers fail in two ways: in their perception of the truth, and in their communicating the truth. They do not see things exactly as they are, nor do they teach them exactly as they see them. But the Spirit of truth does both. O that we were filled with a sense of the glory of the third person of the blessed Trinity. Then we would pray with David, "Thy Spirit is good, lead me into the land of uprightness" (Psalm 143:10).

2. *Let us meditate on the work of the Holy Spirit.* "He will guide you into all truth." In the verses preceding, Jesus had told them what the Comforter would do in the hearts of natural men; "He will convince the world of sin, and of righteousness, and of judgment"; but here He tells them what the Comforter will do for those who are disciples indeed, "He will guide you into all truth". The same sweet promise is repeated, 1 John 2:20. "Ye have an unction from the holy One, and ye know all things." This does not mean that Christians know all worldly knowledge. The apostles themselves, with the exception of Paul, were unlearned and ignorant fishermen of a small inland lake, and many a simple cottage-believer is on his way to glory,

"Who knows, and knows no more, his Bible true".

"Not many wise men after the flesh, not many mighty, not many noble are called." Neither does it mean, that Christians who have the Spirit know all divine things. The disciples were long ignorant of the death of Christ, and of His resurrection; and Paul expressly says, "Now we see through a glass darkly; now I know in part". This is the childhood of the new creature — we speak as a child, understand as a child, think as a child. What then does this promise mean? (i) It means that He will teach you all things needful for your salvation. In smaller matters He sometimes allows you to wander, to teach you your ignorance and weakness; but in things essential to your salvation, He will guide you with His eye. If a mother were guiding her little child through a wood, where there was no danger, she might allow it to stray, now and then, and lose itself, to teach it to keep closer by her side; but if they came to a place where were the dens of wild beasts, she would clasp her child in her arms, and carry it quickly past. So does the good Spirit. In smaller matters He suffers you to err, but not when the safety of your soul is concerned, then He will carry you as on eagles' wings. He will guide you into all truth. That was a sweet word which Jesus spake, "There shall come false Christs and false prophets, insomuch that if it were possible they shall deceive even the elect". Dear believer, whose feet have been set upon the rock, *it is not possible* that you can be deceived as to your eternal salvation. (ii) It means that He is willing to make you know all things. It is your own fault, not His, if you are not guided into all the truth as it is in Jesus: He is an infinite fountain of pure heavenly light; He is willing and able to leave neither sin nor darkness in your soul. Soon you will be filled with the Spirit, and then you will see face to face, and know as you are known, and love as you are loved.

In the following part of the verse, the truth which the Spirit teaches is more fully opened up. "He shall not speak of himself, but whatsoever he shall hear that shall he speak." When Jesus Himself came to this world He came as a Witness. This is His name, Revelation 1:5. "Jesus Christ, the faithful Witness." And He said to Pilate, "To this end was I born, and for this cause came I into the world, that I should bear witness unto the truth". Most men receive His testimony as Pilate did; they say, "What is truth?" and turn away. Still Jesus came to bear witness that men are lost, that God is love, and that there is a way of forgiveness to the chief of sinners. Such is the office of the Spirit of truth, "When the Comforter is come he will testify of me" (John 15:26). O! it is sweet to be taught, by the Spirit, the deep things of God's bosom. "The secret of the Lord is with them that fear him."

Again, "He will show you things to come". This promise was eminently fulfilled in the experience of Paul, when the Spirit showed him so expressly the features of the coming papacy, 1 Timothy 4:1. And in the experience of the beloved John, when, on the lonely rock of Patmos, he was "in the Spirit on the Lord's day".

To all believers it is fulfilled, when amid the bustle, and confusion, and abounding wickedness of their present dwelling, they can calmly, and with holy delight, feed upon the prophecies and promises of the conversion of Israel and of the world.

# 10. Three that Bear Record in Heaven

*There are three that bear record in heaven,*
*the Father, the Word, and the Holy Ghost: and these three are one.*
1 JOHN 5:7

IN VERSES 4 and 5, we see that the only way of overcoming the world is by believing that Jesus is the Son of God. "Be often at Gethsemane, be often at Golgotha"; and so the weakest child of God may trample the world, the devil, and the flesh below his feet. But some may ask, Upon what evidence am I to believe that Jesus is a divine, full, and free Saviour? Here is the evidence, "There are three that bear record in heaven". Oh! that Jesus may breathe upon us while we meditate on *The Heavenly Witnesses.*

1. *The Father.* Jesus often appealed to the testimony of His Father. "The Father himself, which hath sent me, he hath borne witness of me" (John 5:37). One amazing example of this was at His baptism. Jerusalem and all Judea had come out to John to be baptized. The work of the day was nearly done, and it was probably near the evening. The setting sun was pouring his golden rays through the palm trees that skirt the banks of Jordan. John, clothed in his rough garment of camels' hair, stood stern and bold declaring the words of eternal life, while multitudes hung upon his word. Then Jesus came to be baptized. No sooner had He come up out of the Jordan than the heavens were opened, as to the martyr Stephen. Every eye was attracted to heaven; when, behold! a dove descended gently upon the head of Jesus. Every eye now rested upon Jesus; when a still small voice broke upon the silence of evening, like the rushing of the wind through the forest, or like the noise of distant waters. First it spoke to Jesus, "Thou art my beloved Son; in thee I am well pleased". Then it spoke to the listening crowd, "This is my beloved Son, in whom I am well pleased" (Comp. Luke 3:22; Matthew 3:17).

In this way God has confessed Jesus to be His Son, and the Saviour of the world. This testimony was repeated on Tabor's woody summit, and is still unrecalled. That voice is still echoing through the world, and shall do so till the knell of the departing universe, "This is my beloved Son: hear ye him". In this way does the Father point the eyes of all His creatures to Jesus, "Behold the Lamb of God"!

25

2. *The Word.* In courts of law it is not customary to take a man's evidence concerning himself. He would be the very best and most conclusive witness; but man is such a depraved creature that he cannot be trusted in a matter where his own interest is concerned. But Jesus is the blessed Word of God "who cannot lie", and therefore it is quite right and lawful to take His own evidence concerning Himself. Let us meditate on His testimony.

*By His miracles* He declared Himself to be the Son of God, and the Saviour of sinners. "The works that I do in my Father's name, they bear witness of me" (John 10:25). They were all done at His own command and will, not as prophets and apostles wrought their miracles in the name of another. Jesus said, "I will: be thou clean". They were all miracles of mercy; with the exception of cursing the barren fig-tree, and even that, rightly understood, was a miracle of mercy also. All He did showed divine love towards sinners glowing in His bosom. They were all typical miracles; showing forth the glorious salvation which He came to work out. He opened the eyes of the blind, cleansed the lepers, cast out devils, raised the dead. Every one of His miracles did in this way point the weary sinner to Jesus, saying, "Behold the Lamb of God!".

*By His plain declarations* He bare record that He was the Saviour of the world. When He stood beside the well of Sychar, the poor guilty woman of Samaria said to Him, "I know that Messias cometh, which is called Christ: when he is come, he will tell us all things. Jesus saith unto her, I that speak unto thee am he." To a poor guilty worm he plainly revealed Himself.

Again, a poor blind soul at Jerusalem had received sight from Christ. Jesus said to him, "Dost thou believe on the Son of God? He answered and said, Who is he, Lord that I might believe on him? Jesus said unto him, Thou hast both seen him, and it is he which talketh with thee. And he said, Lord I believe." How plainly did He here declare Himself to be the Son of God!

Again, He said to the unbelieving Jews, "I am the bread of life; he that cometh to me shall never hunger, and he that believeth on me shall never thirst". Thus did the blessed Word join in the testimony of the Father, drawing all men to Himself, drawing every eye to behold Him, every heart to cleave to Him. "Behold me, behold me!" "No man cometh to the Father but by me."

3. *The Holy Ghost.* In many ways does the Holy Ghost bear record. At the baptism of Jesus He came down upon Him like a dove. He abode upon Him. He anointed Him for His ministry. He assisted Him to offer up

Himself without spot unto God. But most of all, on the day of Pentecost He bare witness to Jesus. Christ had said, "It is expedient for you that I go away: for if I go not away, the Comforter will not come unto you; but if I go away, I will send him unto you". And so when He came from the hand of the risen Saviour, He showed that Christ was risen indeed. He came in cloven tongues of fire, and every tongue spoke the glory of Jesus, Acts 2. So in every time of the outpouring of the Holy Spirit on the hearts of sinners, there is a fresh testimony that Jesus is the Saviour of the lost. The Spirit always directs the sinner to look to a pierced Christ. "I will pour the spirit of grace and supplications, and they shall look upon me whom they have pierced" (Zechariah 12:10).

Oh! my soul, hast thou believed the record of the heavenly witnesses? "If we receive the witness of men, the witness of God is greater." If a faithful minister says he is willing to receive anxious souls to tell them the way of peace, how many will knock at his door, saying, Sir, what must I do to be saved? And why? Because they believe his word. But why do you not go as confidently to the door of Christ? Does He not say, "Him that cometh unto me, I will in no wise cast out"?

Oh! my soul, behold the guilt, the blackness of unbelief. Words cannot tell the weight of that God-defying sin. "He that believeth not God, hath made him a liar." We shall see better the guilt of this in that day when "the fearful and unbelieving" shall be cast in along with whoremongers and murderers into the lake of fire, Revelation 21:8.

# 11. Gospel not in Word but in Power

*For our gospel came not unto you in word only,*
*but also in power, and in the Holy Ghost, and in much assurance; as ye know*
*what manner of men we were among you for your sake.*

1 THESSALONIANS 1:5

THRICE HAPPY MINISTER who can address his people in these delightful words. Oh! that all our ministers could with truth say this. Why is it not so? Surely if we are determined, like Paul, "to know nothing among them but Christ Jesus and him crucified"; if we are filled with the same Holy Spirit, if we live the same devoted life, and carry the same message night and day with tears, we ought to be able to use these precious words. "He that goeth forth and weepeth, bearing precious seed, shall doubtless come again bearing his sheaves with him." The day of Pentecost was the time of the first-fruits. The day of ingathering is yet to come. The apostles had the former rain. We wait for the time of the latter rain.

1. *Let us meditate on an unsuccessful ministry.* The gospel comes to the people in word only. How often a faithful minister preaches the gospel, and the people seem to drink it in with joy! A beam of natural eloquence lights up all he says, or he has a gentle pathetic strain which rivets their attention. But no saving effects are seen to follow. No hearts are broken, no souls added to the church of such as shall be saved. So it was with Ezekiel: "Lo! thou art unto them as a very lovely song of one that hath a pleasant voice, and can play well on an instrument: for they hear thy words, but they do them not" (Ezekiel 33:32). These are they that receive the word into stony places; they hear the word, and anon, with joy receive it, yet have they not root in themselves, but dure only for a while.

Oh! my soul, art thou contented to receive the gospel in word only? Can a hungry man be fed by the smell of the viands? Or can a beggar turn rich by hearing the sound of money? And can my hungry soul find rest by hearing the tinkling of the gospel cymbals? Alas! it is a fearful thing to drop into hell under the sound of gospel mercy.

But there are some who not only hear the gospel, but know the gospel; and yet it comes to them in word only. How many a child is brought up under godly parents, well catechized in divine truth, well disciplined in the Bible? They understand the gospel scheme. They have all knowledge; no point is new to them. And yet they have no spiritual sight; no tasting and seeing that Christ is good; no rock below their feet; no sitting with great delight under the shadow of the apple-tree. Ah! these are the most miserable of all unconverted hearers. They will sink lower than Capernaum. Ah! how many children of ministers, how many sabbath-school teachers, how many preachers of the gospel may know, that the gospel has come to them in word only, and never in power. Alas! how sad is it to perish pointing to the city of refuge, to preach to others, and then to be a castaway. But there is a more excellent way. Turn we now to meditate on —

2. *A successful ministry.* "Our gospel came unto you in power." What a powerless thing the gospel sometimes appears. The minister is half ashamed of it. The people slumber under its most affecting statements. Again, at another time, the gospel is evidently "the power of God unto salvation". An unseen power accompanies the preached word, and the sanctuary is felt to be the house of God, and the very gate of heaven. Then the word of Jeremiah is fulfilled: "Is not my word like as a fire? saith the Lord; and like a hammer that breaketh the rock in pieces?" (Jeremiah 23:29). Then stout-hearted sinners are awakened. Old, and middle-aged, and little children, are made to cry, What must I do to be saved? An awful stillness pervades the assembly. The arrows of the King of Zion are sharp in the heart of the King's enemies, and the people are brought down under him. Oh! sinner, has the gospel come thus in power to you? Has the hammer of the word broken your rocky heart? Has the fire of the word melted your icy heart? Has the voice that is "like the noise of many waters" spoken peace to your soul?

"Our gospel came unto you in the Holy Ghost." It is He, the third person of the blessed Godhead, that makes the gospel come with power. It was He who "moved upon the face of the waters", when this world was without form and void, and brought life and beauty out of a dead world, Genesis 1:2. It is He that moves over the face of nature still, when the winter is past, and brings the fresh life of spring out of the cold bosom of the ground, Psalm 104:30. But most of all, it is the Holy Spirit's work to take away the vail from the hearts of sinners, so that they turn to the Lord, 2 Corinthians 3:16. The carnal mind has got such enmity to God, the unconverted sinner is so dead in trespasses and sins, the natural man is so stupid in divine things, that there must be the work of the Almighty Spirit — quickening, enlightening, and making willing — before the sinner will cleave to Jesus.

Oh! sinner, has the Holy Spirit come to you? Sweet is the peace which they enjoy who are taught by Him. When it is a dry time, ministers labour in vain; they spend their strength for nought and in vain. They feel like one standing on the sea-shore, speaking to the hard rocks, or the raging waves, or the tameless winds. But when the Holy Spirit comes, the weakest instruments are mighty, "mighty, through God, to the pulling down of strongholds". Oh pray for such a blessed time.

"Our gospel came unto you in much assurance." This is the effect on the soul, when the word comes with power, carried home by the Holy Ghost. The soul thus taught has a sweet certainty of the truth of the great things revealed in the gospel. When a man contemplates the sun, he feels a certainty that it is not the work of man but of God. So when a sinner gets anointed eyes, he sees a glorious beauty and fullness in Christ, so that his heart is filled with a sweet certainty of the truth of the gospel. He does not ask for evidences. He sees enough of evidence in Christ Himself. He says, I am all guilt: thou art Jehovah my righteousness. I am all weakness: thou art Jehovah my banner. I am all emptiness: in thee dwelleth all the fulness of the Godhead bodily. "I am my Beloved's, and my Beloved is mine. He feedeth among the lilies." It is this that fills the bosom with all joy and peace. It is this that gives a sweet sense of forgiveness and nearness to God. It is this that enables us to pray. Now we can say, "My soul shall make her boast in the Lord". "I know that my Redeemer liveth." "Who shall separate me from the love of Christ?" This is the gospel coming in much assurance. Oh! happy minister that can take up these words of Paul, and say, "our gospel came not unto you", etc. That people is thy joy here, and shall be thy crown throughout eternity.

# 12. Saved through Mercy, not Works

*Not by works of righteousness which we have done,*
*but according to his mercy he saved us, by the washing of regeneration, and*
*renewing of the Holy Ghost; which he shed on us abundantly*
*through Jesus Christ our Saviour.*

TITUS 3:5-6

1. *THE WAY OF PARDON*. When a soul is under conviction of sin, he feels that God is angry with him every day. The soul sinks down into a gloomy condition, "the sorrows of death compass him, and the pains of hell get hold upon him". When God visits this soul in mercy, He does it by revealing something in the heart of the Lord Jesus Christ; He makes "the kindness and love of God our Saviour toward man appear" (verse 4). The Spirit pours a beam of light upon the face of Jesus. He shows how He pitied the lost, came for the lost, obeyed and died in the room of the lost, and that the guiltiest of men may freely receive Him as his Saviour. The sinner beholds the Lamb of God, and his bosom is filled with peace in believing. Now this is what is meant in these words, "According to his mercy he saved us".

1. Some souls are seeking salvation "by works of righteousness". You take great pains in religious duties, you read the Word and pray, you feed the hungry, and clothe the naked, in order to make up for past sins, and to lay God under obligation to save you. From these words it is plain that you have mistaken the way to heaven; this way is blocked up; it is "not by works of righteousness which we have done". "If righteousness come by the law, then Christ is dead in vain" (Galatians 2:21).

2. How are we to be saved? It is by "the appearing of the love and kindness of God our Saviour". You think that you must do something to change God's mind toward you, whereas Christ our great High Priest has, by the one offering up of Himself, done all that needs to be done, or that ever can be done, to open the way of reconciliation to God. God is "ready to forgive" (Psalm 86:5). Learn not to look *in*, but to look *out* for peace. You are poring over your dark history, and your still darker bosom; you are straining your eyes to discover some gleam of light there. This is vain. Who ever sought the

31

light of the rising sun by gazing into a dungeon? Look out upon the kindness and love of God our Saviour. It is a discovery of the person, offices, beauty, finished work, and freeness of God our Saviour, that fills the heart with peace, and the mouth with praise.

"My terrors all vanished before His sweet name,
My guilty fears banished, with boldness I came
To drink at the fountain life-giving and free,
Jehovah Tsidkenu is all things to me."

2. *The way of holiness.* "He saved us, by the washing of regeneration, and renewing of the Holy Ghost." (i) It is a "washing". The work of the Spirit on the pardoned heart is called washing, because it is a making clean. The natural heart is polluted and vile; no streams of nature can wash it clean, no good resolutions, or vows, or endeavours can change the carnal heart, Jeremiah 13:23. The Holy Spirit alone can do this. (ii) It is "the washing of regeneration", or of a new birth. It is no outward washing of the body, but an inward change upon the soul; no baptism with water, but baptism with the Holy Ghost. Ah! how often have I washed the body clean; have I ever experienced the washing of regeneration? I was once washed in the water of baptism, have I been baptized with the Holy Ghost also? (iii) It is a constant washing. The water that Christ gives shall be within the soul, "a well of water springing up into everlasting life" (John 4:14). Most places, when well washed, keep clean for a time. Not so the heart of man; it is a vile sink of iniquity. The "river of water of life" must be turned into it, and made to flow perpetually through it. We must be watered every moment. Oh! happy soul that has got the Fountain of living waters within. We do not know our deceitful heart if we do not feel our need of an unceasing well of the Spirit to purify us from all filthiness. (iv) It is "a renewing of the Holy Ghost". When a house has become crazy and insecure, no repairs will do it any good. It must be taken down and built up again. Such a house is the heart of a sinner. It is past all repair. The leprosy of sin is ingrained in the walls of it. It must be taken down and built up again. This is the "renewing of the Holy Ghost". When there has been a long and severe winter the trees stand bare and leafless; they are in a manner dead, and cannot bear fruit. If the winter were to continue they would really die. But when summer breathes upon them again, the juicy sap ascends into the branches in full and mighty stream, "the fig-tree puts forth its green figs, and the vines with the tender grape give a good smell". The face of the earth is renewed, Psalm 104:30. Such a dead

32

plant is the heart of a sinner. A Christless state is the winter of the soul. But when Christ is revealed, when the soul comes into the love of God, when the Spirit is sent forth into the heart, the soul becomes a new creature, and sings, "I am like a green olive tree in the house of God". Lastly, "The Spirit is shed on us abundantly". Christians often complain that there are few drops of the Spirit falling in our day. Alas, there is too great cause for this complaint. Yet in one view it is not true. Wherever there is a single believer, there the Spirit is shed *abundantly*. When I look at the whole world lying in wickedness, and the thousand snares laid for my soul in every path; when I listen to the roaring of the lion who walketh about seeking whom he may devour; and above all, when I look in upon the law in my members warring against the law of my mind, I am tempted to cry, "I shall one day perish by the hand of Saul". If I had legions of angels on my side they could not hold me up. No created arm can keep me from falling. But Jesus says, "My grace is sufficient for thee". He sheds the Holy Ghost abundantly. What a constant dropping of the rain, what a constant springing of the well, what a full inflowing of the river of God is needed to hold up my helpless soul. Glory to God for an indwelling Sanctifier. "Now unto him who is able to keep me from falling, and to present me faultless before the present of his glory with exceeding joy, to the only wise God our Saviour be glory and majesty, dominion and power, both now and ever. Amen."

# 13. Saviour Praying for the Comforter

*And I will pray the Father, and he shall give you another Comforter,*
*that he may abide with you for ever.*
JOHN 14:16

HOW MUCH of the majesty of Christ shines in these words! What a divine sweetness breathes in them! He knows his own mind, he knows the mind of his Father, he knows the mind of the Spirit, and, therefore, he speaks with a holy certainty. I will pray, the Father shall give, the Spirit will abide with you for ever. We should receive His words with the same sweet certainty as that with which they were spoken.

1. *Observe what Christ will do.* "I will pray the Father." This shows that Christ is not dead. He was dead, but He is now alive for evermore. The dead do not pray; the lips that are sealed in death are silent lips. But Jesus says, "I will pray the Father". He looks beyond his agony in the garden, and on the cross; He looks beyond His rocky sepulchre; and, as if He had nothing to do but to step into the presence of His Father, He says, "I will pray the Father".

Again, this shows the constancy of Christ's love. When a friend is going away to a far land — an "inner friend" — a praying friend, we say to him as we are going to the ship, "Now you will never forget us", and he says, "No I never will, I will pray for you". O! such a friend is Christ. He is one born for adversity, a friend that sticketh closer than a brother. At times we are cast down when we think of His glory, and our meanness; of His being the very Sun of heaven, and we a vile worm on the earth; but be not faithless but believing. I will never forget you, He says, even when I am at the right hand of the Father, I will pray for you.

2. *Observe what the Father will do.* "He shall give you another Comforter". We learn from these words the certainty of the gift of the Holy Spirit. How confidently Jesus speaks, "No man knoweth the Father but the Son, and he to whom the Son shall reveal him". If an angel had come and said, the "Father shall give you another Comforter", we might have doubted; for, how does an angel know what the Father will give? But Jesus is "the true and faithful Witness", He had "come from God, and went to God"; and He says with a divine boldness, "The Father shall give". Ah! how many Christians seem never to have received the Comforter. How many have no sweet sense of forgiveness. How many have no close walk with God. Ministers constantly bless their flocks, saying, "The communion of the Holy Ghost be with you all". How few seem really to possess it. Why is this? It is because of unbelief. You do not fully realize this truth, "We have an advocate with the Father, Jesus Christ the righteous". You do not believe that the Father delights to give the Spirit, in answer to the prayer of His Son. You do not live upon that promise, Isaiah 49:8, "In an acceptable time have I heard thee".

Again, observe that word, *"another* Comforter". Jesus was the first Comforter. He came "to comfort all that mourn"; His words were all "good words, and comfortable words"; His blood was peace-speaking blood. He

34

had comforted the disciples by the way, by the well, and on the stormy sea. But now He must go His way to Him that sent Him. He leaves this word behind, "I will pray the Father, and he shall give you *another* Comforter". "He that spared not his own Son, but delivered him up for us all, how shall he not with him, also, freely give us all things." Enter into this argument, O my soul! He that gave the first Comforter for sinners will surely give the second Comforter to His dear children.

3. *Observe what the Comforter will do.* "Abide with you for ever." Jesus and His Spirit are one. He knew what is the mind of the Spirit. He also knew what is in man — the unbelieving, inconstant, unholy heart of man, and yet he says the Comforter shall abide with you for ever. Sometimes a young believer is cast down by this thought, "How do I know that my faith shall not fail me; the vail of unbelief may cover my heart again, perhaps in the hour of temptation, perhaps in a dying hour". Here is the answer, Jesus will pray, the Father will give, and the Comforter will abide with you for ever. Observe this in a singular instance, Luke 22:31. "Simon, Simon, Satan hath desired to have you, that he may sift you as wheat, but I have prayed for thee that thy faith fail not." Be not afraid, only believe, all things are possible to him that believeth. He that was the Author will be the Finisher of your faith.

Sometimes a young believer is sadly cast down by a discovery of the plague of his own heart. When he looks into the smoking volcano that is in his own bosom, he begins to tremble lest after all he become a cast-away. Take these two directions: (i) Be humbled in the dust under your body of sin and death, but do not despair. Paul had the same, and all true Christians have the same. Make this resolution your own, "Resolved never to give over, nor in the least to slacken my fight with my corruptions, however unsuccessful I may be". (ii) Believe in the Comforter. Keep your eye fixed on Christ, on His wounds out of which the blood flowed, that cleanseth from all sin; on His lips that pray so sweetly for His own (Song 5:16). Wait for "that holy Spirit of promise". He alone can make you holy; and He will do it, for faithful is He that promised.

# 14. Argument to Prayer for the Spirit

*If ye then, being evil, know how to give good gifts
unto your children; how much more shall your heavenly Father give the
Holy Spirit to them that ask him?*

LUKE 11:13

JESUS DESIRES all His disciples to pray for the Holy Spirit. He knows
that we cannot believe at the first, nor continue believing without this
precious gift. He knows that our soul cannot live, love, resist the devil,
mortify the deeds of the body, nor overcome the world, without this living
water; therefore does He urge His people to ask, seek, and knock. He is still
saying to poor sinners, "If thou knewest the gift of God, and who it is that
saith to thee, Give me to drink, thou wouldest have asked of him, and he
would have given thee living water" (John 4:10).

1. *Earthly fathers, who are evil, give good gifts to their children.* This is a
fact in human nature. The most wicked fathers are often kind to their off-
spring. In some countries it is true, Satan has shown his infernal power in
destroying the parental affections, so that the Hindoo mother has been
known to plunge her sickly infant into the Ganges, or even to hurry it, while
yet alive, into a grave dug with her own hands, and to trample the ground
over it with her own feet. "The dark places of the earth are full of the habita-
tions of cruelty." In general, however, there is, even in the bosom of savage
men, a chord of tenderest love toward their little ones. The wild Indian of
America will bring home from the woods the most brilliant feather to deck
the brow of his prattling boy; and the rude Greenlander will brave the icy
blast to provide a scanty meal for his tender children. You must break a
father's heart in pieces, before you can break asunder that mysterious bond
of love that binds him to his child. Earthly fathers who are evil give good
gifts to their children.

2. *How much more shall God, who is a good Father, give the Holy Spirit.*
God excels an earthly father in two respects:

(i) *He is wise,* "the only wise God". Earthly fathers are short-sighted
men. They do not know the wants of their children, nor do they know
the best time and way of supplying these wants. They often give to their

36

children when they should withhold, they pamper their humours, and spoil their dispositions; they often withhold when they should give, and provoke their children to fretfulness. But God is a wise Father. "The Father of spirits" knows our frame, and remembers that we are dust. He knows our minutest wants, and He knows the very best time and way of supplying them. Above all, He knows our need of the Holy Spirit. He knows that we are naturally dead in trespasses and sins. He knows that a vail is over our hearts — He knows that our faith is weak — and that our enemies are too many for us, and too strong. He knows the temptations and afflictions to which we are called. He knows the manner and measure of the Spirit's help which we need to keep us from falling.

(ii) *God is love.* God has a natural love to a soul in Christ. Earthly fathers love their children, but O how coldly compared with God's love. In Isaiah 49:15 it is preferred above a mother's love: "Can a woman forget her sucking child, that she should not have compassion on the son of her womb? yea, they may forget, yet will I not forget thee." There is no love in this world like a mother's love. It is a free, unbought, unselfish love. She cannot account for it. You cannot change it. You must break to pieces the mother's heart before you will change it. It is the fullest love with which a creature can love. She loves with all her heart. But the love of God to a soul in Christ is far above a mother's love. It is a love ingrained in His nature, and God must change before His love can change. It is a full love. The whole heart of the Father is as it were continually showered down in love upon the Lord Jesus. And when a sinner comes into Christ the same love rests upon that soul (see John 17:26). When the sun showers down its beams on the wide ocean, and on a little flower at the same time, it is the same sunshine that is poured into both, though the ocean has vastly larger capacity to receive its glorious beams. So when the Son of God receives the love of His Father, and a poor guilty worm hides in Him, it is the same love that comes both on the Saviour and the sinner, though Jesus is able to receive infinitely more. In Psalm 103:13, God's love is compared to a father's love: "Like as a father pitieth his children, so the Lord pitieth them that fear him." His love combines all the tenderness of a mother's, and all the wisdom of a father's love. How surely then will He give the Holy Spirit to every one of His children that ask Him. Far more surely than an earthly father gives bread to his hungry children. This is good news for my weary soul. I am like David in the wilderness (Psalm 63 title), "My soul thirsteth for thee, my flesh longeth for thee in a dry and thirsty land, where no water is". "My soul followeth hard after thee;

thy right hand upholdeth me." All my grace comes from thee. Thou didst begin the good work in me when I was an enemy, wilt thou not carry it on, now that I am a child? Thou didst pour down the Spirit when I was like the dry ground, wilt thou not water me every moment now that I am a plant, though a feeble one, of thine own planting? Hear the divine answer, O my soul, and be still! "I will heal their backsliding, I will love them freely, for mine anger is turned away from him. I will be as the dew unto Israel" (Hosea 14:4-5).

# 15.  The Peace of Zion's Children

*All thy children shall be taught of the Lord; and great shall be*
*the peace of thy children.*
ISAIAH 54:13

WHEN THE JEWS are brought again to Zion, and converted to God, they will be an example of a people, "all taught of the Lord". God says, Jeremiah 31:34, "They shall all know me, from the least of them even unto the greatest of them". And again, Isaiah 60:21, "Thy people shall be *all* righteous". They are to be the first example of a "righteous *nation*". In some of our well-ordered parishes, we see a people all taught of man; but, ah! how much ignorance, deceit, and wickedness are lying below the surface. But all the children of Zion shall be taught of the Lord, and, therefore, they will be a people of great peace, and great holiness.

Such is the case of spiritual Zion at this moment. They are all taught, not of man, nor of angel, but of the Lord, and their peace passeth all understanding.

1. *Meditate on the great teacher, the Lord.* He alone knows divine things as they are. Ministers have but glimpses into the eternal world. They see but little of sin, of the shortness of time, of the depth of hell, of the love of God, of the person, work, and grace of Christ. Therefore they cannot teach

38

effectually. Books also are infinitely imperfect. The best of them are but sparks from the Bible, mingled with human darkness. But the Lord knows all things as they are. "All things are naked and laid open to the eyes of him with whom we have to do." He knows our infinite guilt; hell and destruction are before Him. He knows the Son. "No man knoweth the Son but the Father." He knows, "The love of Christ, that passeth knowledge". He then can make it known. O my soul hast thou been taught of the Lord? Again, He alone can teach the heart. Man can speak to the ear, to the understanding, to the memory, God alone to the heart. The reason why human teaching does not convey saving light to the soul is, that the heart is dead. The carnal mind is enmity against God, and against everything that comes from God; and, therefore, when the truth is presented, the worldly heart draws the mind away from beholding it. But when the Lord is teaching, He touches the heart, and it melts under His hand. He awakens concern in the dead soul, so that the person runs to hear the word preached. He makes the soul willing in the day of His power. He makes salvation, by Christ, clear to the mind, and sweet to the heart, in the same happy moment. None can teach like God. He can teach a child, or an idiot, or an old man. Is any thing too hard for the Lord? "O send forth thy light and thy truth, let them lead me, let them guide me."

2. *What is divine teaching?* It is not mere head-knowledge of divine things. Many have great knowledge of the Bible, have read it all, studied much of it, learned much of it by heart; they know the Catechism well, they have a just notion of divinity; some have great knowledge of books, of Boston, and Willison, and Flavel; some may be great judges of sermons, able to discriminate between legal and evangelical preachers; alas! all this may be, and more, without one spark of divine teaching. Alas! how many ministers have there been like the finger-post that points the way, but does not go. No doubt Judas had a clear knowledge of divinity, and could preach well, yet Jesus said he was a devil. We know that Satan has great knowledge of the Bible, and yet he only trembles.

What then is divine teaching? It is God giving the soul a sense of the wondrous beauty, excellence, and sweetness of the way of salvation by Christ. "Open thou mine eyes that I may behold wondrous things out of thy law." Take an example in one of the most eminent saints that ever lived. "The first instance that I remember, of that sort of inward sweet delight in God and divine things, that I have lived much in since, was on reading these words, 1 Timothy 1:17, 'Now, unto the King eternal, immortal, invisible, the only wise God, be honour and glory for ever and ever. Amen.' As I read these words, there came into my soul, and was as it were diffused through it, a sense of the glory of the divine Being; a new sense, quite different from anything I ever experienced before. Never any words of Scripture seemed to me as these words did. I thought with myself, how excellent a Being that was, and how happy I should be if I might enjoy that God, and be rapt up to Him in heaven, and be as it were swallowed up in Him for ever! I kept saying, and as it were singing over these words of Scripture to myself; and went to pray to God that I might enjoy Him; and prayed in a manner quite different from what I used to do, with a new sort of affection. But it never came into my thought that there was anything spiritual or of a saving nature in this. From about that time, I began to have a new kind of apprehensions and ideas of Christ, and the work of redemption, and the glorious way of salvation by Him. An inward sweet sense of these things, at times, came into my heart; and my soul was led away in pleasant views and contemplations of them."

Ah! this is divine teaching. This is the teaching that brings us to the foot of Christ, like the woman which was a sinner. Before, we are perplexed about coming to Christ, believing on Christ, closing with Christ; but now it is all sweet and easy; we cannot but believe on Jesus. This is teaching that fills the bosom with all joy and peace. It gives "great peace", "peace like a river", "joy unspeakable and full of glory". This is the teaching that sanctifies. A man may have the head-knowledge of an angel, and the heart of a devil. But when God touches the heart He makes all things new.

# 16.  Saving Faith the Gift of God

*By grace are ye saved through faith;*
*and that not of yourselves; it is the gift of God.*

EPHESIANS 2:8

MOST MEN try to lay God under a debt to save them. They work for salvation instead of working from it. They "go about to establish their own righteousness". In this way worldly people seek eternal life: "What shall we do, that we might work the works of God?" (John 6:28). Although in words they renounce all pretence of any worth in themselves or in their duties, yet they have a secret hope of recommending themselves to God by their decency, sobriety, and religious performances. In this way those who have a little concern for their souls, like the young ruler, seek for eternal life: "Good Master, what good thing shall I do, that I may have eternal life?" (Matthew 19:16). His earnest desire was to make himself appear righteous before God. In this way, also, those who are under the deepest concern often wander in search of pardon and peace. Perhaps there may be traces of this feeling in the anxious question of the poor jailor, "Sirs, what must I do to be saved" (Acts 16:30); and in the piercing cry of the prostrate Saul, "Lord, what wilt thou have me to do?" (Acts 9:6). Certain it is that self-righteousness is the worst and longest-lived viper in the human breast. Most men under convictions are very unwilling to throw away all *self-confidence.* They are not willing to despair of ever being fair in the sight of God in themselves. They shrink back from the idea of being lost and undone, for anything that they can do. They do not like to venture to lie helpless and without a plea at the feet of a sovereign God. How solemn to a sinner in such a state should these words be, "By grace ye are saved through faith; and that not of yourselves; it is the gift of God"!

1. *Salvation is by grace.* When a man chooses an apple off a tree, he generally chooses the ripest, the one that promises best. It is not so with God in choosing the soul He saves. He does not choose those that have sinned least, those that are most willing to be saved; He often chooses the vilest of men, "to the praise of the glory of his grace". This is proved by the instances given in the Bible of brands plucked out of the burning. Why did God

41

choose Manasseh, who "caused his children to pass through the fire", set "a carved image in the house of God", and filled Jerusalem with the blood of holy men, while many of his deluded people, who had sinned far less, perished? (2 Chronicles 33). Why did God save Zaccheus the hoary-headed swindler, "the chief of the publicans"? (Luke 19:1-10). Why did Jesus tell the Pharisees, "the publicans, and the harlots go into the kingdom of God before you"? Why did Jesus enter into the pearly gates of paradise with a poor thief, who had never done anything but sin up to his last hour? (Luke 23:43, comp. Matthew 27:44). Why did He leave the other thief, who was no worse than his fellow (both were hell-deserving), to sink into perdition within an arm's length of an Almighty Saviour? All these things happened unto them for ensamples, to show us that God saves according to the good pleasure of His will, not for our goodness, but to show His own free adorable grace.

The same thing is proved by the experience of every child of God. Who that has ever "tasted that the Lord is gracious", does not feel a response in their bosom to the declaration of a simple believer, "Had He not chosen me before I was born, He had never seen reason to choose me afterwards". There was nothing in me to attract the love of God. "Behold, even to the moon and it shineth not, yea, the stars are not pure in his sight; how much less man that is a worm, and the son of man which is a worm." He loves what is pure, holy, heavenly; but "I am carnal, sold under sin". There was everything in me to drive God away. "God is angry with the wicked every day" (Psalm 7:11). He was angry with me. His whole nature abhorred me, for I was under Adam's sin; I was shapen in iniquity; every member of my body, every faculty of my soul, had been only the servant of sin. Yet He came over all these mountains to my soul. I said, Art thou come to torment me before the time? I desire not the knowledge of thy ways. But He made me willing in the day of His power. Glory, glory, glory, to the Father who chose me, the Son who died for me, and the Spirit who quickened me. Salvation is of the Lord, and it is all of grace.

2. *Salvation is through faith.* When David Brainerd was under conviction of sin, the corruption of his heart was dreadfully irritated by this, that faith alone was the condition of salvation. Of this very text he used to say, "It is a hard saying: who can bear it?". Another thing that kept him in misery was this, "I could not find out what faith was, or what it was to believe, and come to Christ. I read the calls of Christ to the weary and heavy laden, but could find no way that He directed them to come in." This is a difficulty

42

which almost every inquiring sinner feels. It is probable that Satan often uses it as a fiery dart to keep poor sinners away from Christ. The only way really to know what faith is, is to experience it. In one part of the word it is described as *"knowing"*. "This is life eternal, that they might know thee the only true God, and Jesus Christ whom thou hast sent" (John 17:3). A true realizing knowledge of God, and of Christ as the sent of God, is saving faith. Have I this knowledge, O my soul? I was born like a wild ass's colt. God was not in all my thoughts. I did not like to retain God in my knowledge. But it pleased God to reveal His Son in me. Flesh and blood could not reveal Him unto me, but my Father who is in heaven. He has opened to me the way of salvation, so that I see its wisdom, excellency, and freeness; I cannot but believe, and this I humbly trust is that faith which is the gift of God.

Again, it is described as *discovering the beauty and excellency of Christ:* "In that day shall the branch of the Lord be beautiful and glorious, and the fruit of the earth shall be excellent and comely for them that are escaped of Israel" (Isaiah 4:2). A real discovery of the glory, suitableness, and freeness of the Lord Jesus Christ in the soul, is saving faith. Natural men know what it is to get a discovery of a beautiful countenance, and the natural heart immediately glows with admiration. None but believers know what it is to get a discovery of the fair face of Him who is "fairer than the children of men", and to have the heart filled with all joy and peace in believing. Has this discovery been made to me? Can I say, "Whom, having not seen, I love; in whom, though now I see him not, but believing, I rejoice with joy unspeakable and full of glory"? Once I saw no form nor comeliness in Jesus, no beauty that I should desire Him. But He came like a roe or a young hart, leaping on the mountains, skipping on the hills. He stood behind our wall, He looked in at the window, *showing Himself* through the lattice. He showed me His hands and His feet pierced for sinners. He showed me that there was room beneath His shining righteousness. He showed me His heart, the same yesterday, to-day, and for ever; and now I cannot but say, He is to me beautiful and glorious, excellent and comely. If there were ten thousand other ways of pardon, I would pass them all by, and flee to Him. He is altogether lovely. This I trust is saving faith, which is the gift of God.

> "Amazing grace! (how sweet the sound!)
> That saved a wretch like me:
> I once was lost, but now am found;
> Was blind, but now I see.

'Twas grace that taught my heart to fear,
And grace my fears relieved;
How precious did that grace appear
The hour I first believed!

Through many dangers, toils, and snares,
I have already come;
'Tis grace has brought me safe thus far,
And grace will lead me home."

# 17. True Believers the Sons of God

*But as many as received him,*
*to them gave he power to become the sons of God,*
*even to them that believe on his name.*

JOHN 1:12

WHEN THE LORD OF GLORY came to this world, the most despised and rejected Him. Yet all did not. Isaiah cried, "Who hath believed our report, and to whom is the arm of the Lord revealed?". And yet in a few verses after he adds, "He shall see of the travail of his soul, and shall be satisfied" (Isaiah 53:1, 11). In like manner, John in this chapter tells us, that when Jesus came, "the darkness comprehended him not"; "the world knew him not"; "his own received him not". Still, a little flock did receive Him. Their eyes were opened to behold His glory, their hearts to feel His love. They left their earthly all, and followed Him, they hung upon His lips, kept His sayings, walked in His steps, put on His righteousness, drank in His spirit; and "to them he gave power to become the sons of God". There always has been, and always will be, a hidden church. As David was never to want a son to sit upon his throne, so David's Son and David's Lord never shall want souls over which to reign. As in Noah's day of almost universal corruption, and in Elijah's day of dark idolatry, there were some hidden ones that knew and loved the Lord; so in our day, in the darkest parishes of Scotland, you will find some hearts that kindle at the name of Jesus. In countries sunk in the darkness of popery, you will find some heaven-taught souls groping their way to heaven by the strait gate and the narrow way. Christ will never want a vineyard on earth on which to show His love and care. He will never want a witnessing church to proclaim His grace. "Upon this rock I will build my church, and the gates of hell shall not prevail against it" (Matthew 16:18).

How clearly these words show that to receive Christ is the same as to believe on His name. Many souls find great difficulty in knowing what faith is. Satan seems to make great use of this in some hearts, in order that he may divert their anxious soul from the great object of faith to look at the workings of their own mind. The Bible makes no difficulty in the matter. At one time it is described as *coming* to Jesus: "I am the bread of life, he that cometh to me shall never hunger, and he that believeth on me shall never thirst" (John 6:35). Again, it is called *a laying hold:* "Who have fled for refuge to lay hold upon the hope set before us" (Hebrew 6:18). In another scripture it is called *submitting:* "They have not submitted themselves to the righteousness of God" (Romans 10:3). In other parts of the Word of God it is called *looking to Jesus, calling* upon the name of the Lord, *hearing* that the soul may live, *knowing, cleaving* to the Lord. In one and all of these the meaning of God is, that the heart is made willing to be justified through the blood and obedience of the Lord Jesus. O! it is the truest and most lasting joy in the universe when Christ is fully revealed to the soul, and when the excellency of the way of salvation by Christ is made manifest; the heart is often so filled that the tongue cannot speak. It is "joy unspeakable, and full of glory".

Sinner, have you received the Lord Jesus Christ? Has your heart melted at the sight of the heaven-provided Saviour? Have you known the gift of God? Have you seen and delighted in the *finished work* of Christ? If Christ had to come and die, you might say, perhaps He will not go through with it. But He has done it. It is more than eighteen hundred years since He agonized in Gethsemane, and poured out His soul upon the cross. "It is finished." His whole work, as Surety in the place of sinners, is finished. The whole undertaking is completed. Nay more, God has accepted it. He has declared it from heaven: "This is my beloved Son in whom I am well pleased" — and that any sinner is welcome to draw near by Jesus. O! I am willing to be found

45

in Jesus, let your soul reply; I am willing to stand under the shelter of the one Mediator to all eternity. What satisfies God satisfies me. "Who shall condemn? It is Christ that died."

But what good shall I obtain by receiving Christ? Hear the divine answer: "As many as received him, to them gave he power to become the sons of God." An awakened soul is seeking only rest, peace with God, forgiveness of sins. But Christ gives far more. He gives the child's place in the father's love. We are by nature children of wrath, a generation of vipers, children of the wicked one; but the moment we consent to put on the glorious righteousness of Immanuel we become adopted sons of God: "God sent forth his son, made of a woman, made under the law, to redeem them that were under the law, that we might receive the adoption of sons." Sinner! do you know what it is that God offers you in the gospel? Though you are a viper, under the curse of the broken law, and your heart more like Satan than God, yet the holy God offers you a place in His bosom. He sent forth His Son to make room for you, to take you into the son's place. What are all the joys of sin compared with this? What are earthly titles compared to this? Sounding brass and a tinkling cymbal. Surely you must be deceived by the god of this world, if you are willing to remain a child of the devil rather than become a child of God.

There is still fuller blessing contained in these words. Those who receive Christ receive power to become adopted sons. This is blessed, this is wonderful. But those who receive Christ receive power to become real sons — sons by a new birth. It is good to be an adopted son, but ah! to be a real son of God, having the same spirit, features, joys, this is the full bliss of being a Christian. When a rich man adopts a beggar boy into his family, and takes him for a son, he not only clothes him, and feeds him, but he educates him as his child. He puts him under a teacher to rid him of old habits, to put a new spirit in him, the spirit of his own child. This is what God does with all that receive Christ. When a sinner flees to Christ, God not only puts the best robe on him, and embraces him, and seats him at His table, but he sends forth the Spirit of His Son into his heart. The same almighty Spirit that dwelleth in His own bosom, and in His Son, the Spirit that was given to Jesus without measure, He sends into the poor pardoned sinner's heart, to make him a son indeed, "born not of blood, nor of the will of the flesh, nor of the will of man, but of God". Surely if men knew what God is willing to do for them in Christ, they could not so lightly esteem the Rock of their salvation. O sinner! God is willing to take out your old alienated heart, and to give you the heart of one of His own weaned children. He is willing to give you the Spirit of Christ, to change you into His image, to make you like Him now and in eternity. Surely it may be said to every soul that despiseth Christ, "Woe unto thee, O Jerusalem! wilt thou not be made clean? when shall it once be?" (Jeremiah 13:27).

# 18.　Help Thou Mine Unbelief

*And straightway the father of the child cried out, and said with tears,*
*Lord, I believe; help thou mine unbelief.*
MARK 9:24

HOW VERY SMALL was the faith with which this man came to Christ. It was like a grain of mustard seed. Twice we read of Jesus expressing wonder at the great faith of the poor worms that applied to Him. When the centurion came to Him in behalf of his beloved servant who was sick, he believed that Christ was willing and able to heal him, though he lay beneath a sinful roof. "Jesus marvelled at so great faith" (Matthew 8:5-13). When the Syrophenician woman cried after Him in behalf of her child, she would not be turned back by His long silence, or by His seemingly rough words; she saw deep into His heart of grace, and waited for an answer of peace, till Jesus cried, "O woman, great is thy faith, be it unto thee even as thou wilt" (Matthew 15:21-28).

Another time a leper came, and as he kneeled said, "Lord, if thou wilt thou canst make me clean". This was little faith. He believed the power of Jesus; he was not sure of His willingness. He thought He might be willing, for he came and applied to Him; still he was not sure, and said, If thou wilt. With holy majesty Jesus rebuked his unbelief, and granted his desire: "I will, be thou clean" (Matthew 8:3). But far weaker than all these was the faith of this unhappy father; "If thou canst do anything, have compassion on us, and help us". Alas, that ever such words should be spoken to the Lord of glory. He in whose hand our breath is, and whose are all our ways — He by whom all things were created that are in heaven, and that are in earth — He whose name is Jehovah-Rophi, "The Lord that healeth thee", was standing before him, and yet his faith could reach no higher than that, "If thou canst do anything". And yet Jesus did not cast the unbelieving man away from Him. Jesus never can deny that word, "Him that cometh unto me, I will in no wise cast out". He sent him home a happy father with his child made whole. These things were written for our admonition, upon whom the ends of the world are come. How evil unbelief appears in another, and yet how little do I perceive the same dishonouring thoughts of Christ when they lurk in my own bosom. I feel as if I never could use such language to Jehovah-Jesus; and yet how many times in the day I doubt both His love and His power. How often, when guilt is on my conscience, I doubt whether He be entirely willing to be the Mediator between God and such a sinful wretch as me. How often, in an hour of temptation, when the passions are roused, I doubt whether He be able to subdue such a heart as mine. How often these words are the language of my heart: "If thou canst do anything, have compassion on me, and help me." And yet for all our unbelief, He doth not send us empty away. Faith, as a grain of mustard seed, obtains everlasting benefits, Luke 17:6. Do not let me then keep away from Christ, because my faith is small. Though He had to call His disciples, "Ye of little faith", yet that did not hinder Him from rebuking the winds and the sea for them, and there was a great calm, Matthew 8:26. In like manner though my name may be, "Thou of little faith", to the end of life's troubled journey, yet will I go to Him with such faith as I have, and He will in no wise cast me out.

But observe the prayer of the anxious father, "Lord, I believe, help thou mine unbelief". O! surely this was a groan dictated by the Spirit of supplications. Never was prayer better timed, or better expressed. The Author of faith stood before him — to whom could he go for faith but unto Christ? Faith is the gift of Jehovah Jesus, John 17:2. He in His kingly power, riding through the world, sends out His arrows, and brings down the people under Him, Psalm 45:5. He not only brings gold for our ransom, and white raiment to cover our nakedness, but He brings in His hand, to the door of sinners, eye-salve to anoint our eyes, that we may see, Revelation 3:18. He was not only wounded for our transgressions, and bruised for iniquities, but He bids us reach forward our finger, that He may guide it into the prints of the nails, and reach forward our hand, that He may guide it to His wounded side. He was not only the Rock cleft for sinners, but by His Almighty power He puts us into the cleft of the rock, and hides us there, Exodus 33:22.

Would that all the church of Christ were taught this prayer, "Lord, I believe, help thou mine unbelief", or that other, "Increase our faith" (Luke 17:5). Two precious things are contained in it. A sense of our want of faith, and a clear knowledge of the fountain whence living faith must flow. Few people know how small their faith is. In a Christian land, sitting under a lively ministry, surrounded by warm-hearted Christian friends, the feelings are fanned into a glow, and the believer thinks that his faith is strong and full. But let providence call that believer to a foreign land, where —

"The sound of the church-going bell
These valleys and rocks never heard,
Never sighed at the sound of a knell,
Nor smiled when a sabbath appeared."

Let him wander among those that never pray to Jesus, like Abraham in the land of the Canaanites, or let him lie on a sick bed with none to wait on him that know the Saviour, then he will begin to learn by sad experience that warm feelings are not faith — that faith in Jesus is like a grain of mustard seed in his bosom. O it is a painful but a blessed lesson to be taught how weak our faith is. It makes us trust less to our feelings, and less to friends, and makes us cleave closer to Christ as our all in all.

But if it be good to know how little faith we have, it is better far to know what an overflowing fountain Jesus is. He is "Alpha and Omega, the beginning and the ending". He is "the Author and the Finisher of our faith". He anointed our eyes at the first, and made us see men as trees walking. He alone can anoint them more fully, that we may see all things clearly. He alone can help our unbelief. He can cover all the sin of it, for O it is crimson sin. He can remove it by fuller discoveries of Himself. "My Beloved is like a roe, or a young hart". On Judah's hills the gazelle bounds with amazing ease and graceful swiftness over the most rugged rocks. It is its very nature to spring from crag to crag. So easily, swiftly, and agreeably to His gracious nature does the Lord Jesus reveal Himself to the souls that wait for Him. Often by a single visit the unbelief of half a lifetime vanishes, and the soul cries out with adoring joy, "My Lord, and my God". Wait on the Lord Jesus, O doubting soul. Be of good courage, and He shall strengthen thine heart. "It is good that a man should both hope and quietly wait for the salvation of the Lord" (Lamentations 3:26). Often look beyond the blue sky to Him who sits on the right hand of God, and cry out with tears, "Lord, I believe, help thou mine unbelief".

# 19. Strengthened with Might by the Spirit

*That he would grant you, according to the*
*riches of his glory, to be strengthened with might by his Spirit*
*in the inner man; that Christ may dwell in your hearts by faith; that ye,*
*being rooted and grounded in love, may be able to comprehend*
*with all saints what is the breadth, and length, and depth,*
*and height; and to know the love of Christ, which*
*passeth knowledge, that ye might be filled*
*with all the fulness of God.*
EPHESIANS 3:16-19

HOW REMARKABLE are the prayers of Paul! He used to pray for individuals whom he loved by name. Without ceasing, the names of Timothy and Philemon were upon his heart, 2 Timothy 1:3; Philippians 4. He prayed for believers whom he had never seen, Colossians 1:9, 2:1. He prayed for all true saints, Ephesians 6:18, 24. He wrestled with continual sorrow of heart for the Jews, Romans 9:1, 10:1. In how remarkable a manner he prayed, "without ceasing", "day and night", "with joy", "with thanksgiving", with humility "bowing his knees". How large were his requests! He opens his mouth wide, that God may fill it. In Romans 15:13 he prays: "Now the God of hope *fill* you with *all* joy and peace in believing." In 1 Thessalonians 5:23 he prays: "And the very God of peace sanctify you *wholly*," etc. So in these words he asks for amazing gifts. God only can fully comprehend the vast meaning of such a prayer. The words of man seem to be too narrow to express his large desires. These are "groanings that cannot be uttered", the intercession of the Spirit through the mind and heart of Paul. None but God could answer it.

O that all ministers could pray like Paul. Probably no man ever lived who was the means of saving so many souls as Paul. Probably no minister was ever made the instrument of bringing his people to such a height of holiness as Paul. How was this? Look at his prayers for an answer. Consider their frequency, their urgency, their vastness. It was on his knees Paul fought the good fight of faith, and obtained grace for his own soul, and for all the churches. Such a man would be a blessing to the whole world. "O Lord, teach us to pray." There are three principal petitions here, each one growing out of the other.

1. *Consider the last petition,* verse 19, "That ye might be filled with all the fulness of God". This is the sum and end of all his prayers for them. Indeed it is the chief end of man. The great object of the gospel is to bring poor empty sinners to be filled with all the fulness of God, to be like an empty vessel cast into a vast ocean, to be filled with all the fulness of His love, of His presence, of His Spirit, of His joy, of His likeness. This Adam would have been had he persevered in holiness. This we become when united to Christ, and shall be to all eternity. This David panted after, "My soul thirsteth for God, for the living God" (Psalm 42:2). This David, in some measure, enjoyed: "Whom have I in heaven but thee, and there is none on earth whom I desire beside thee" (Psalm 73:25). Certain it is that the believer's God can draw near, and reveal Himself, and fill the soul in a way that worldly men never thought of. He can fill the heart with a *sense of His love.* One dear Christian could say, "My soul hath been compassed about with the terrors of death, the sorrows of hell were upon me, and a wilderness of woe was in me, but blessed, blessed, blessed be the Lord my God, He hath brought me to a place of rest, even to the sweet running waters of life". Another dear Christian, of whom President Edwards writes, experienced such clear and lively views of Christ that "her soul did, as it were, swim in the rays of Christ's love like a little mote swimming in the beams of the sun that come in at a window". The same person, speaking upon the most deliberate consideration, could say, that "what was enjoyed in a single minute of the whole space, which was many hours, was worth more than all the outward comfort and pleasure of the whole life put together". O! that Christians now were filled with these drops of the fulness of God. He can fill the soul with *His holiness.* A natural man has not a spark of God's holiness. He may be pleasant, amiable, and of a natural integrity, but he has none of the "living water". The moment a soul is united to Christ, the same Holy Spirit who dwells in the bosom of the Father dwells also in him. "I will put *my* Spirit within you" (Ezekiel 36:27). The believer becomes "a partaker of the divine nature" (2 Peter 1:4). He becomes "a partaker of his holiness" (Hebrews 12:10). He does not become as holy as God, but the same stream that flows through the divine bosom flows through the soul that is one with Jesus. O to be holy as He is holy, blessed as He is blessed, pure as Christ is pure. O to be filled with all the fulness of God.

2. *Consider the second petition,* verses 17-19, "That Christ may dwell in your hearts by faith, that ye, being rooted and grounded in love, may be able to comprehend with all saints what is the breadth, and length, and depth, and height; and to know the love of Christ, which passeth knowledge". This appears to be one vast petition expressed twice over, that they may have a calm, abiding, realizing view of Christ and His love. If any man were to ask, How shall I come to be filled with the fulness of God? The answer will be found in this prayer; you must come first to an abiding believing knowledge of "the love of Christ which passeth knowledge". Keep the eye of faith continually fixed on Jesus, on His glorious person, "fairer than the children of men"; on Jesus your Prophet, having "the tongue of the learned to speak a word in season to them that are weary"; on Jesus your Priest, "through the eternal Spirit offering himself without spot unto God"; on Jesus your King, reigning from sea to sea in the hearts of His own, and winning many crowns in the conversion of sinners. Behold Him, behold Him. Keep your eye and heart upon Him, keep the arms of faith around Him, so "that Christ may dwell in your heart by faith". A tree takes a firm hold of the ground by its thousand roots; the winds shake but cannot remove it, so let your heart "be rooted and grounded in the love of Christ", then you may calmly view the vastness of that love.

When a man is first awakened he does not know much of his sin, and cannot know much of the love of Christ; but when rooted and grounded in Christ, and the Spirit breathes in the heart, he then begins to comprehend with all saints, and to know the love of Christ that passeth knowledge. Observe "the breadth and length of it": "As far as the east is from the west, so far hath he removed our transgressions from us" (Psalm 103:12). Compare Leviticus 16:22. So broad and so long is the love of Jesus. Observe the depth of it: "He being in the form of God, thought it no robbery to be equal with God, but emptied himself," etc. (Philippians 2:6). Measure from the throne of glory to the cross of Calvary, or to the rocky sepulchre — so deep was the love of Christ. Observe the height of it: "To him that overcometh will I grant to sit with me on my throne" (Revelation 3:21). Measure how far it is from the lowest hell to the throne to which Christ will raise us; so high was the love of Christ. "It passeth knowledge". It is like a vast ocean, and our heart is like a little creek upon the shore; we embrace the ocean, but we cannot measure it; we shall know more of it in eternity; we never shall know it all, for "it passeth knowledge"; and it gives "a peace that passeth all understanding".

3. *Observe the first petition,* verse 16. "That he would grant you, according to the riches of his glory, to be strengthened with might by his Spirit in the inner man". If any man were to ask, How shall I come to that abiding believing knowledge of the love of Christ? The answer is to be found in this petition. The Father must grant you His free Spirit. Every word is precious — "That he would grant you". The gift of the Spirit at first is of free grace. When He breathes on the dry bones in the open valley, it is of freest mercy. And so every further work of the Spirit on the heart is of free grace. O what need have we to pray, "Cast me not from thy presence, neither take thy Holy Spirit away from me".

But has God enough to supply our need? Yes, He has "riches of his glory", unsearchable riches. Just as He has inexhaustible treasures of rain and dew to water every green herb, so He has infinite treasures of the Spirit all ready to be poured into the hearts of His needy people. But what will His Spirit do for me? "He will strengthen you with might in the inner man." Your eye is dim, and cannot see afar off. He will anoint it that you may see the King in His beauty. Your heart is dead and stony. He will quicken and soften it that eternal things may impress you. Your faith is like a bruised reed. He will strengthen you with might, so that you shall hold Christ, and not let Him go. It is true of the Spirit as of the Father, that "he giveth power to the faint, and to them that have no might he increaseth strength".

# 20.   The Faithfulness of God

*God is faithful, by whom ye were called unto the fellowship of*
*his Son Jesus Christ our Lord.*
1 CORINTHIANS 1:9

THE ANXIETIES of a faithful pastor never end in this world. First he is anxious that his people be brought to Christ, and then he is anxious that they be kept abiding in Him to the end. What a fountain of consolation is this text while he looks upon those, of whom in his heart he has the sweet persuasion that they are "sanctified in Christ Jesus, and called to be saints", and repeats these words in his heart, "God is faithful, by whom ye were called unto the fellowship of his Son Jesus Christ". It is this sweet truth, the faithfulness of our covenant God, that is a rock to the pastor's soul, and makes him feel that those who are now "dearly beloved, and longed for", will soon be "his joy and crown". But not only to the pastor, to the flock also, especially in time of temptation, affliction, and desertion, these words are like "the snow of Lebanon, or the cold flowing waters from another place". Sometimes it pleases God to withdraw His comfortable presence from the soul, chiefly to humble us in the dust, to discover some unmortified corruption, or to lead us to hunger more vehemently after Him. Such was David's state when he said in his heart, "I shall now perish one day by the hand of Saul" (1 Samuel 27:1). And again, when he wrote the 42nd Psalm. Such was the feeling of Job when he said, "the arrows of the Almighty are within me"; and again, "Oh that it were with me as in months past, as in the days when God preserved me; when his candle shined upon my head, and when by his light I walked through darkness" (Job 29:2-3). In such an hour as this, when the feeling of distance from God is almost insupportable, ah! how cheering, how full of nourishment, what a heavenly cordial may this word in the hand of the Spirit be: "God is faithful, by whom ye were called unto the fellowship of his Son Jesus Christ our Lord."

1. *Believers are called to share with Christ.* To have fellowship with another, is to have things in common with him. Thus in Acts 4:32, it is said of the first Christians, that they were "of one heart and of one soul, neither said any that ought of the things which he possessed were his own, but *they had all things in common"*. They had all their goods in common, they shared all they had with one another. This is what John desired to see amongst Christians in spiritual things, "That which we have seen and heard declare we unto you, that ye also may have *fellowship* with us" (1 John 1:3). The same expressions is used here, "Ye are called unto the *fellowship* of his Son". How strange, that a creature of sin and shame should be called to share with God's dear Son. Yet so it is; He shared our flesh and blood with us, that we might share His throne with Him.

(i) *We share with the Son in His justification.* Once Jesus was unjustified. Once there were millions of sins laid to His charge. Men, devils, nay, even His holy Father, hurled their fierce accusations at Him. He stood silent. He could not answer a word. Although "he did no sin, neither was guile found

54

in his mouth"; yet He had agreed to bear the sins of many, and therefore, He was dumb under every accusation. "It was exacted, and he was made answerable". This was His chief agony in the garden, and on the cross, that at the bar of God He was unjustified; "He was numbered with the transgressors". His only comfort was, "He is near that justifieth me" (Isaiah 50:8). He knew that His trial would be short and that He would overcome. The hour of darkness is now past. The wrath of God has all fallen upon Him. The thunder clouds have spent their lightnings on His head. The vials of God's anger have emptied their last drops upon Him. He is now justified from all the sins that were laid upon Him. He will bear the scars to all eternity, Revelation 5:6; but not another drop of agony shall ever fall upon His soul. When He comes a second time it is "without sin" (Hebrews 9:28). Have you the Son? Do you believe the record that God has given concerning His Son? Do you with purpose of heart cleave to the Lord Jesus? then you share with Him in His justification. You suffered in His suffering, you obeyed in His obedience, you died in His death. You are as much justified as Christ is. You have as little to do with the guilt of your past sins as Christ has. There is as little guilt lying upon you as upon God's dear Son. The vials of wrath have not another drop for Christ, and not another drop for you. "By Jesus all that believe are justified from all things" (Acts 13:39).

(ii) *We share with the Son in His Father's love.* When Jesus was about to leave this world, He said to His disciples, "I leave the world and go to the Father". When He died He cried, "Father into thy hands I commend my spirit". When He entered into heaven and passed up the opening ranks of the adoring angels, the Father said, "Thou art my Son, this day have I begotten thee"; as if He had said, Never till this time did I see thee so worthy to be called my Son. Ah! it was a blessed exchange when He left the frowns and curses of the world for the embrace of His Father's arms; when He came from under the outpoured wrath of God into His full eternal love and smile; when He left the crown of thorns for the crown of glory. Such is the change of every poor sinner in the moment that he is persuaded and enabled to embrace Christ. Dost thou believe with all thine heart that Jesus is the Son of God? Can you say you have fled for refuge to Christ? Then you share with Christ in His Father's love. Christ says, "I ascend unto my Father and your Father, and to my God and your God" (John 20:17). God is as much your Father as He is Christ's Father. Your God as Christ's God. The Father loves you with the same full, unchanging, soul-satisfying love, with which He loves Jesus (see that never to be forgotten prayer, John 17:26). Oh! what a blessed change for an heir of hell to become an "heir of God, and a joint heir with Christ" (Romans 8:17). For one who deserved, and still deserves, to share with the devil and his angels, to share with Christ that sits at the right hand of God. Oh! to inherit God, to have a son's interest in God! Eternity alone can reveal the full meaning of that word, "Heir of God, and joint heir with Christ".

2. *God is faithful to souls in Christ.* "God is faithful, by whom ye are called unto the fellowship of his Son." When a soul is in affliction, tempta-tion, or desertion, his cry is, "The Lord hath forsaken me, and my God hath forgotten me". Sometimes this feeling approaches to actual despair. Here is a rock for the soul to lean upon, "Christ is the same yesterday, to-day, and for ever", and "God is faithful" who called us to share with Christ. Hearken to the voice of the great Shepherd, "My sheep hear my voice, and they follow me, and I give unto them eternal life, and they shall never perish, neither shall any pluck them out of my hand. My Father which gave them me is greater than all, and none is able to pluck them out of my Father's hand." Satan desires to have you. The world are laying snares for you. Your own wicked heart would sometimes be for leaving the hand that has saved you. But *"none* is able to pluck you out of the Father's hand". Hearken to the Father's own word, "Thou art my servant, I have chosen thee and not cast thee away" (Isaiah 41:9). The soul united to Jesus is not like the grass, but like the palm tree. Even in old age he shall bear fruit, he shall be full of sap and flourishing. "To show that the Lord is upright: he is my rock, and there is no unrighteousness in him" (Psalm 92:15). At the very time when Zion was saying, "My God hath forgotten me", God had her walls engraven on His hands, Isaiah 49:16. Look still to Jesus, oh! deserted soul. The love of God shines unchangeably on Him. Abide in Him and you will abide in the Father's love. Your afflictions may only prove that you are more imme-diately under the Father's hand. There is no time that the patient is such an object of tender interest to the surgeon, as when he is bleeding beneath his knife. So you may be sure if you are suffering from the hand of a reconciled God, that His eye is all the more bent on you. "The eternal God is thy refuge, and underneath are the everlasting arms."

# 21.    Called with an Holy Calling

*Who hath saved us, and called us with an holy calling,*
*not according to our works, but according to his own purpose and grace,*
*which was given us in Christ Jesus before the world began.*

2 TIMOTHY 1:9

THERE ARE TWO WAYS in which men are called to believe the gospel.
There is an outward and an inward calling, an earthly and a heavenly calling.
All believers are "partakers of the heavenly calling" (Hebrews 3:1).

The outward call comes to all who hear the gospel sound: "Many are
called, but few chosen." Every time the *church bell* rings it is a call. It says,
"Come away sinner, thy sabbaths are numbered. Eternity is at hand. God's
people are hastening to the house of God, God's stewards are dealing out the
bread of life. Sinner do not stay behind; Jesus is ringing for thee, inviting
thee, wooing thee. If thou wouldst but listen, it would sound as joyfully as a
marriage bell." Ah! there are multitudes in Scotland who hear no more of
the gospel than the bell, and that will be enough to condemn them in the
great day. *The open church door* is a call. It seems to say, "Strive to enter in at
the strait gate, for many shall seek to enter in and shall not be able". "Go ye
to them that sell, and buy for yourselves," lest the bridegroom come and the
door be shut.

> "Come in, come in,
> Eternal glory thou wilt win."

*The lighted windows* of the church at evening are a solemn call. They cry in
your ears, "Jesus is the light of the world". "Yet a little while is the light with
you. Walk while ye have the light, lest darkness come upon you." Jesus hath
lighted a candle, and is sweeping the house, and seeking diligently to find
lost pieces of silver. *"The village spire* that points the way to heaven," is a
silent call. It says, Look up stedfastly into heaven, and see the glory of God
and Jesus standing on the right hand of God. "Seek those things which are
above. Set your affections on things above, not on things on the earth." *The
voice of the preacher* is a call. It says, "Repent and believe the gospel, for the
kingdom of heaven is at hand". "We are ambassadors for Christ, as though

57

God did beseech by us, we pray you in Christ's stead, be ye reconciled unto God." *Every tract* given in at your door is a divine call. It says, "I have a message from God unto thee". "Behold I stand at the door and knock." *Every leaf of your Bible* is a call. It says, "Search the scriptures. I am able to make thee wise unto salvation through faith which is in Christ Jesus. I am given by inspiration of God, and am profitable for doctrine, for reproof, for correction, and instruction in righteousness." *The death of every unconverted friend* is a loud call. It says, "Except ye repent, ye shall all likewise perish". "It is appointed unto all men once to die, and after death the judgment." "Prepare to meet thy God." It may truly be said of every sinner that shall read these words, that you are *now* called, warned, invited to flee from the wrath to come, and to lay hold on Christ set before you. If you have not got enough to save you, you have enough to condemn you.

But all who are in Christ have received the inward call. All, who like Timothy, have "unfeigned faith", and have received "the Spirit of power, and of love, and of a sound mind", have been "saved and called with a holy calling". This is the work of the Holy Spirit; and therefore it is called a *holy calling.* It is the call of the unseen Almighty Spirit who sweetly inclines the will, and melts the heart of the sinner. It is there *a saving call.* When Jesus said to Matthew, "follow me", the Spirit breathed upon his heart, and made him willing: "He arose and followed Jesus." When Paul preached to the Thessalonians, he gave the outward call. Had Paul stood alone, they would have remained as hard as the rocks that dash back the waves of the Aegean Sea. But the Spirit breathed upon their hearts, and so the "gospel came not unto them in word only, but in power, and in the Holy Ghost, and in much assurance" (1 Thessalonians 1:5). When Paul preached at Philippi by the river's side, many a Grecian matron had the outward call. His words fell pleasantly upon their ears. Still all remained unmoved but one; one heart was opened, a foreigner whose dark eye told that she came from the sunny plains of Asia. "The Lord opened the heart of Lydia" (Acts 16:14).

O sinner! do not think that your reading or hearing the gospel will of itself save your soul. Do not think that because you have a Bible, a minister, and a place in the house of God, that you are therefore on the way to heaven. Remember God must save you, and call you with an holy calling. If you are not quickened from above, your outward calls will only be the savour of death unto death to your soul. It will be one of the chief miseries of hell to remember the texts and sermons that you heard on earth, when you would not come to Christ and have life.

58

Bless God, you who have been "saved and called with an holy calling", for it is "not according to your works, but according to His purpose and grace which was given us in Christ Jesus before the world began". Every saved soul can say, "He hath not dealt with me after my sins, nor rewarded me according to mine iniquities". He has called me out of darkness into marvellous light, from under wrath and curse to pardon and peace with God, from death unto life. How many He has passed by that were no worse than me. But He has been willing to make known the riches of His glory on me, a vessel of mercy which He had afore prepared unto glory. How sure my sinful soul is of glory. He calls *from* heaven, and calls *to* heaven. "Whom he did predestinate, them he also called, and whom he called, them he also justified, and whom he justified, them he also glorified." "Bless the Lord, O my soul."

# 22.    Chosen to Salvation

*But we are bound to give thanks alway to God*
*for you, brethren, beloved of the Lord, because God hath from the beginning*
*chosen you to salvation, through sanctification of the Spirit,*
*and belief of the truth.*

2 THESSALONIANS 2:13

WHEN TRAVELLING through popish countries, where the people bow down to images of wood and stone, and where God's Word is forbidden, the mind of a believer turns to the fearful words in the preceding verses with a feeling of unutterable sadness; and, again, when the mind wanders from these desolate regions to the little flock of dear believers in happy Scotland, it realizes something of the joyful feeling with which Paul wrote these words — "But we are bound to give thanks alway to God for you, brethren, beloved of the Lord" (verse 13).

1. *We are here taught that God is sovereign in choosing the souls that are saved.*

(i) *He is sovereign in choosing men, and not rebel angels.* We read in the Bible of two grand apostacies from God. The first took place in heaven. Lucifer, son of the morning, one of the brightest cherubs that stood round the throne, rebelled through pride along with myriads of the holy angels. "They kept not their first estate, but left their own habitation." "God spared them not, but cast them down to hell, and delivered them into chains of darkness, to be reserved unto judgment" (2 Peter 2:4). The next rebellion was in paradise. Man believed Satan rather than God, and ate of the forbidden fruit. "By one man's disobedience many were made sinners." Both of these families sinned against the same God, broke the same holy law, fell under the same curse, and were condemned to the same fire. Now it pleased God, in infinite compassion, to provide a way of pardon for some of these lost creatures. He determined to save some "to the praise of the glory of his grace". But whom shall he save — men or rebel angels? Perhaps the unfallen hosts of heaven pleaded that their once brother angels should be taken, and men left. They might have said that the angelic nature was higher and nobler, that man was a worm. "O the depth of the riches both of the wisdom and knowledge of God!" He spared not the angels. He passed by the gate of hell. He raised no cross of Calvary there. "He took not on him the nature of angels; but he took on him the seed of Abraham" (Hebrews 2:16).

(ii) *He is sovereign in choosing the countries that have the light of the gospel.* All nations are equally lost, and vile in the sight of God. "He hath made of one blood all nations of men for to dwell on all the face of the earth." And yet how differently has He dealt with different peoples. Why did God choose Israel to be a peculiar treasure to Himself, and to have the oracles of God committed to them? Was it because they were more righteous than others. No; that is expressly denied: "Understand, therefore, that the Lord thy God giveth thee not this good land to possess it for thy righteousness; for thou art a stiff-necked people" (Deuteronomy 9:6). Neither was it on account of their greatness: "The Lord did not set his love upon you, nor choose you, because ye were more in number than any people; for ye were the fewest of all people; but because he loved you" (Deuteronomy 7:7). Again, why has China, with its teeming millions, been walled around for centuries, and left to the darkness of its vain idols? Why has India been left under the cruel chains of Hindooism? Why has Africa been almost given over to witchcraft and superstition? Why has the fair face of Europe been almost given over to the delusions of the man of sin; and why has our own bleak island been chosen to be so long the brightest repository of the truth in all the world? Are we better than they? No, in no wise. There are sins committed among us that would make the heathen blush. "His way is in the sea." "He hath mercy on whom he will have mercy; and he hath compassion upon whom he will have compassion."

(iii) *He is sovereign in choosing the most unlikely persons to be saved.* You would have expected that most of the rich would have been saved. They have most time to study divine things; they are not harassed by the fears of poverty; they can procure all advantages. And yet hear the Word of God: "Hath not God chosen the poor of this world rich in faith, and heirs of the kingdom" (James 2:5). Again, you would have thought God would have chosen the wise and learned, to be saved. The gospel is a subject of deep wisdom. The Bible is written in ancient languages, hard to be acquired. And educated men are generally free from prejudices, to which the common people are subject. And yet hear the word of our Lord: "I thank thee, O Father, Lord of heaven and earth, because thou hast hid these things from the wise and prudent, and hast revealed them unto babes. Even so, Father, for so it seemed good in thy sight." You would have thought that surely God will save the most virtuous people of the world. He is a God of purity, who loves what is holy; and though none are righteous, no, not one, yet some are much less stained with sin than others. Surely He will take these. What says the Lord Jesus to the Pharisees? "The publicans and harlots do enter into heaven before you." The blameless young ruler is left to go away sorrowful, whilst the King of glory enters in at the pearly gate of the New Jerusalem with a thief washed in His blood by His side.

If my soul is saved, am I not bound to give thanks? If ministers are bound to thank God for the free salvation of their people, how much more are we bound to praise Him ourselves for saving us. I am no better than a rebel angel. Devils never rejected Christ as I have done, and yet He passed them by and saved me. I am no better than a Chinese or a Hindoo, and yet grace has passed millions of them, and come to me. I was no better than the sinners round me, perhaps worse than most, and yet I trust I can say, "Thou hast delivered my soul from the lowest hell". Glory to God the Father, that He chose me before the world was. Glory to Jesus, that He passed by millions and died for me. Glory to the Holy Spirit, that He came out of free love and awakened me.

61

2. *We are here taught that God chooses the means as well as the end.* "He hath chosen us unto salvation, through sanctification of the Spirit, and belief of the truth." The first step that God chooses His people to come to, is "belief of the truth". God does not choose men to leap from their sins into glory. But He sends the free Spirit to anoint their eyes, to melt their hearts, to persuade and enable them to embrace Christ freely offered in the gospel. A simple heart-felt belief of the truth, is the first mark that we have been chosen to salvation. "All that the Father giveth me, shall come to me." Have I come to Jesus? Then I know that I am one of those whom the Father gave to Him before the world was. Do I really believe the truth as it is in Jesus? Then God has chosen me to salvation. The second step that God chooses His people to come to, is "sanctification of the Spirit". It is written, "After that ye believed, ye were sealed with that Holy Spirit of promise" (Ephesians 1:13). The moment the soul cleaves to the Lord Jesus, the Holy Spirit takes up His abode in that bosom; He abides there for ever. He changes the cage of unclean birds into a temple for Jehovah's praise. He makes the soul all glorious within. He destroys the dominion of sin; He fills, quickens, renews the whole inner man. Have I received the Holy Ghost? Has that heavenly seal been applied to my heart, impressing upon me the features and the mind of Jesus? Have I the sanctification of the Spirit? Then I have the clear evidence that my calling and election are sure. I can look back to my election before the world was; and forward to my salvation when the world shall be passed away. How foolish is the presumption of those who say, "If I am not elected, I cannot be saved, whatever I do; and if I am elect, I shall be saved in whatever way I live". The simple answer is this, Whether you are elect or not, *you cannot be saved without believing the truth, and being sanctified by the Spirit.* What is written in the Lamb's book of life, I do not know; but what is written in the holy Bible, I do know, that "he that believeth shall be saved; he that believeth not shall be damned". And "without holiness, no man can see the Lord".

# 23. Quickened Together with Christ

*But God, who is rich in mercy, for his great love*
*wherewith he loved us, even when we were dead in sins, hath quickened us*
*together with Christ, (by grace ye are saved).*

EPHESIANS 2:4-5

WHAT A FEARFUL DISCOVERY do these words give of what was once the condition of all true believers? "We were dead in sins." The apostle classes himself with the Ephesian believers in the humbling confession. The most living and burning saint, who now tunes his harp before the throne of the Lamb, was once a dead soul. This is the true condition of all unconverted men at this moment; they are dead in sins. Even our highly-favoured country is like the valley which Ezekiel saw full of bones: "And he caused me to pass by them round about; and, behold, there were very many in the open valley, and, lo, they were very dry" (Ezekiel 37:2). *The understanding* of a natural man is dead: "He is wise to do evil, but to do good he has no knowledge" (Jeremiah 4:22). "There is none that understandeth, there is none that seeketh after God" (Romans 3:11). The mind is often clear and penetrating on earthly things, but it is dark and dead in heavenly things. *The heart* is dead. True, it is alive toward worldly friends, and worldly objects. In pursuit of their lusts "they have made ready their heart like an oven, while they lie in wait". But set the loveliest of all beings before them, the precious corner-stone, the desire of all nations, the pearl of great price; and their heart is not affected, it melts not, it moves not, it loves not; it is dead. *The conscience* is dead. They feel wrongs done against themselves or against their neighbours, but they do not feel wrongs done against God, or against Christ, or against the Holy Spirit: "Unto them that are defiled and unbelieving is nothing pure; but even their mind and conscience is defiled" (Titus 1:15). In some the death of the conscience is total, so that they are past feeling, "having their conscience seared as with a hot iron". How many swearers can pour out their oaths, without once imagining that they are striking at the throne of God. How many can put away the gospel message, without feeling that they are making God a liar. How many can come unconverted to the Lord's table, without once thinking that they are crucifying Christ afresh,

63

and putting Him to an open shame. In such cases their "consciences are seared as with a hot iron".

Turn we now to consider the blessed change that has been wrought in the heart of every believer: "He hath quickened us together with Christ." It was a solemn scene when Jesus stood beside the rocky sepulchre of Lazarus. It was a little way from the village of Bethany, embosomed in its fig and almond trees. Martha and Mary stood weeping, and many Jewish friends beside them. They had rolled away the stone from the mouth of the cave, and as the Saviour looked into the dark silent tomb He cried, "Lazarus come forth. And he that was dead came forth bound hand and foot with grave clothes, and his face bound about with a napkin." This was giving life to the dead. A still more marvellous scene, compared to which this is but as the drop before the thunder shower, shall yet take place upon this earth. "The hour is coming in which all that are in the graves shall hear his voice, and shall come forth, they that have done good unto the resurrection of life, and they that have done evil unto the resurrection of damnation." When the voice of Christ is heard, then from every lonely church yard, from the deep caverns of the sea, and from silent battlefields, the myriads of sleeping dead shall rise and come forth. It will be a day of joy to some, and of woe to others, joy and woe unspeakable. But more wonderful, even than this, is the quickening of the soul in conversion. It is spoken of in these words, "The hour is coming, and now is, when the dead shall hear the voice of the Son of God, and they that hear shall live" (John 5:25). In every part of the world where the Spirit accompanies the preaching of the gospel, this secret, silent resurrection of dead souls is going on every day, little noticed by men, though well known in heaven, and in hell. When the Spirit comes He gives life to the dead conscience; He makes it accuse and condemn the sinner, so that He feels lost and undone. He gives life to the understanding, anointing the eyes wth eyesalve, so that the sinner sees the way of pardon provided by God. He gives life to the heart, melting it, and persuading the sinner to cleave to Jesus; and so He "quickens us together with Christ". The Spirit thus raises the soul out of its grave, looses his grave clothes, namely, worldly lusts and attachments, and lets him go free. "What shall we then say to these things? If God be for us, who can be against us." If He quickens my soul, then no power can keep it dead. Truly, the guilt, indwelling sin, temptations, and spiritual enemies of my soul often confound me. But I pray to know "the exceeding greatness of his power to us-ward who believe" (Ephesians 1:19).

But what is it in the bosom of God that moves Him to quicken a dead soul? The answer is to be found here: "God who is rich in mercy, for his great love wherewith he loved us, (by grace ye are saved)." The free rich grace of God is the fountain from which the quickening Spirit flows. When God came to save Paul he found him dead in sins. There was nothing in the heart of Paul to draw God to visit his soul. But He came because He was rich in mercy, and out of the great love wherewith He loved him, by grace He saved him. There is nothing lovely or attractive about the dead, especially if they have been long dead. The coldness, the want of motion, the paleness, the want of animation, is dreadful. The corruption is abominable. And so Abram says, over the remains of his beloved Sarah, "Give me a possession of a burying-place, that I may bury my dead out of my sight" (Genesis 23:4). So there is nothing amiable to the eye of a holy God in a dead soul. The coldness, the insensibility, the corruption is loathsome, in His pure sight. And yet He came to the dead soul of Paul, and gave it life. And every soul that now rejoices in the love of God can say, I was polluted in mine own blood, when He passed by and said unto me, Live; yea, he said unto me, when I was in my blood, Live, Ezekiel 16:6.

There is good news for those who feel themselves loathsome as the putrid dead. You may be quickened, for such were all believers once. Good news for those who feel helpless as the dead. The Lord can quicken such. And He is rich in mercy; "He willeth all men to be saved, and to come unto the knowledge of the truth". He is not willing that any should perish, but that all should come to repentance. In Him compassions flow. He is ready to forgive. One poor soul who had long been tempest-tossed under the conviction of a life time of sins, was brought to full peace in Christ by meditating on the first verse of the fifty-first Psalm: "According unto the multitude of thy tender mercies, blot out my transgressions." She said, "I will just put the multitude of His tender mercies over against the multitude of my sins". And so she found rest for her soul. Surely this soul, and all who have been thus saved by free sovereign grace, will have cause to join in Rowland Hill's favourite hymn:

> "And when I'm to die,
> Receive me, I'll cry,
> For Jesus hath loved me, I cannot tell why.
> But this I can find,
> We two are so joined,
> He'll not be in glory, and leave me behind."

# 24.    New Creatures in Christ

*Therefore, if any man be in Christ,*
*he is a new creature: old things are passed away;*
*behold all things are become new.*

2 CORINTHIANS 5:17

WHAT IS IT to be in Christ Jesus? It is a very remarkable expression, and occurs very frequently in the Word of God. Paul speaks of Andronicus and Junia his kinsmen, "who also were in Christ before me" (Romans 16:7). He says, that he counted all things but dung, that he might "win Christ, and be found in him" (Philippians 3:9). And he speaks of dear departed believers, as those who "sleep in Jesus" (1 Thessalonians 4:14). The meaning of this blessed expression is, that those who have fled to Christ, are reckoned with by God as if they were a part of Christ. His crucifixion is reckoned theirs; His spotless obedience is reckoned theirs. God sees no iniquity in them. He looks upon them in the face of His Anointed. Just as Christ was in us when He stood in our place, and was covered over with our sins so completely that none of His holiness appeared, so we are in Christ when we submit to His precious righteousness, and are so covered, that none of our sins appear in God's pure sight. How plainly was this sweet truth taught to our first parents after the fall: "Unto Adam, and to his wife, did the Lord God make coats of skins, and clothed them" (Genesis 3:21). How plainly did He teach them that they could not come naked and guilty into His presence, neither could their own rags of self-righteousness cover them, but the snowy clothing of a slain Lamb must be their raiment, neither have they strength to put it on themselves, but God must clothe them. Thus they were taught what it is to be in Christ Jesus.

When Jacob came to his father Isaac in the goodly sweet-smelling raiment of his elder brother, and he came near to his father, and his father kissed him, and smelled his raiment, and blessed him, this was a dark shadow of the way in which a sinner comes to the Father, Genesis 27:18. Here only is the great difference: God is not deceived at all, but of His own free will, most truly, righteously, and by consent of our Elder Brother, clothes us in the sweet-smelling raiment of Jesus, so that we can sing, "He hath clothed me with the

66

garments of salvation, he hath covered me with the robe of righteousness, as a bridegroom decketh himself with ornaments, and as a bride adorneth herself with jewels" (Isaiah 41:10). In the parable of the vine (John 15) Jesus said to the disciples, "Abide in me, and I in you. As the branch cannot bear fruit of itself, except it abide in the vine; no more can ye, except ye abide in me". He teaches us the need of a vital and continued union to Himself. It is not enough once to consent to be washed in my blood, and clothed with my righteousness, you must remain thus, even until death. And herein consisted all the peace and joy of the first believers; they constantly abode in Christ. This was their answer to all accusations, "Christ hath died", "I am crucified with Christ". Herein consisteth all my joy. Blessed be the day when first I was found in Christ. Whenever I am in myself before God, then comes darkness, accusations of conscience terrify me, the curses of the law threaten me, the smallest temptation is too strong for me, my soul is like a rolling thing before the whirlwind. But the moment I am again made willing to hide in the wounds of the great Mediator, to be covered with the bright shining folds of His "garment down to the foot", that moment the accusations of conscience are hushed, the thunders of Sinai die away, I sit like the maniac at the feet of Jesus, clothed, and in my right mind, and a still small voice whispers within my breast, "Ye are become dead to the law by the body of Christ, that ye should be married to another, even to him who is raised from the dead, that we should bring forth fruit unto God" (Romans 7:4).

What is the result of being in Christ Jesus? "If any man be in Christ Jesus, he is a new creature; old things are passed away, behold! all things are become new". A divine change takes place upon that soul more wonderful than the creation of the world, a change brought about by Him who calleth the things that are not as though they were. Indeed this change is begun before the soul submits to Christ, for nothing less than Almighty power can melt the rocky heart, and bend the stubborn will to relish the gospel way of salvation. But it is after a man is brought to Christ that the change is manifested.

1. *He becomes a new creature in understanding.* No man dares to think until he is at peace with God. The mind of a natural man shrinks back from contemplating the realities of God and of the eternal world. The understanding is busied about things seen and temporal, or else about unseen things apart from God; but all that is divine and holy in the universe, or in other words, all that is truly worth knowing, is a field into which the unconverted soul dare not enter. "The natural man knoweth not the things

of the Spirit of God." When a soul is made willing to take Jesus as his mediator, and comes into pardon and peace with God, then he begins to think. A new world is opened up to him, the ocean of divine truth stretches out before him, and the verdant hills of immortality rise up to view. The treasures of wisdom and knowledge hid in Christ, and the glories of the three-one Jehovah now fix the heart. The Holy Spirit renews the soul in knowledge after the image of Jesus. A new life of the understanding is begun in that soul. "I am unable to express the actings of my soul as I feel them (says Andrew Lindsay), yet I am helped to conceive a little of them by the springs which are in the way from my home; as those springs, though small, have some water in them, so I trust it is with my soul; the water in some of these springs is covered with grass and weeds, so is the sight of this life hid from me, at times, by the corruption of my heart; but as the water appears on a man's removing the weeds with his hands, so does this life by a new manifestation. And as the water continues in these springs, now in August when great pools are dried up, so I hope the life of God will continue in my soul, because the love of Christ is unchangeable." Happy soul! This is the experience of a new creature in Christ Jesus.

2. *He becomes a new creature in his affections.* No man truly loves till he come to Christ. "Love is of God, and every one that loveth is born of God, and knoweth God. He that loveth not knoweth not God, for God is love." Before Paul fled for refuge to lay hold on Christ, he was an old creature in his affections. "I verily thought with myself that I ought to do many things contrary to the name of Jesus of Nazareth" (Acts 26:9). His heart was like a bow bent against Christ and His cause. He hated the humbling truths of the gospel. When God's faithful witnesses were put to death, he gave his voice against them. But when he came to Christ he was made a new creature. Never, perhaps, did such burning love to Christ ever glow in a human bosom as in Paul's: "What mean ye to weep and to break mine heart? for I am ready not to be bound only, but also to die at Jerusalem for the name of the Lord Jesus." And now what tender compassion breathes through his soul toward the little flock of Christ: "Being affectionately desirous of you, we were willing to have imparted unto you, not the gospel of God only, but also our own souls, because ye were dear unto us." He is a new creature in love. He has got the same stream of love in his heart that springs eternally from the bosom of God. O sinner! this is what God will make thee if thou art willing to be found in Christ. Remember, none but new creatures will ever enjoy the new heavens and the new earth wherein dwelleth righteousness.

# 25.    Ministry of Reconciliation

*All things are of God, who hath reconciled us
to himself by Jesus Christ, and hath given to us the
ministry of reconciliation.*

2 CORINTHIANS 5:18

IN THE PRECEDING VERSE it is written, "If any man be in Christ Jesus, all things are become new" in that soul, and here we are told whence all this change proceeds: "And all things are of God". The beginning, the carrying on, and the perfecting of the glorious work of regeneration in the soul, is the work of Jehovah; so that every new creature can sing, "The Lord will perfect that which concerneth me; thy mercy, O Lord, endureth for ever; forsake not the work of thine own hands" (Psalm 138:8). In a still wider sense these words are true, "All things are of God". He is the fountain of being: "In the beginning God created the heavens and the earth. And God said, Let there be light, and there was light." All creatures flow from Him, and will ultimately show forth His highest praise. Hearken to the song of the four and twenty Elders, as they cast their crowns before the throne: "Thou art worthy, O Lord, to receive glory, and honour, and power; for thou hast created all things, and for thy pleasure they are, and were created" (Revelation 4:11). He is the fountain of providence. Every drop of water in the air, or in the river, or in the ocean, performs its appointed course. The myriads of insects that flutter in the sunshine, all fulfil His will. And every man, angel, and devil, only fulfil the eternal counsel of the blessed Jehovah: "All things are of God." The natural heart rages against this truth, but it is like the raging of the foam upon the everlasting rocks — the purpose of the Lord it shall stand. But the true meaning of the words is, that all things of the new creation in the soul are of God. It is God who freely, sovereignly, and from eternity loves the soul that is to be saved: "I have loved thee with an everlasting love, therefore with lovingkindness have I drawn thee." It is God who guides the soul under the ministry where he is to be awakened, He prepares the way to the heart, and at length, when His blessed time is come, He sends the word home with power. It is God who keeps the awakened soul from going back to the world, from taking rest in any refuge of lies, or from being

69

offended at Christ. It is God who reveals His Son in the heart, as He did to Paul: "It pleased God, who separated me from my mother's womb, and called me by his grace, to reveal his Son in me." This is a work peculiarly divine; nature cannot help in it. Man cannot accomplish it. It is God who now fills the soul with the Holy Spirit, and He persuades the sinner most freely and heartily to leave old sins, old habits, old companions, and to follow Jesus in the way. All this amazing change, more wonderful than the creation of the world, more durable than the whole material universe, is the work of God alone: "All things are of God." Ah yes! when my guilty soul shall stand washed, and justified, and sanctified before the throne of God, when I shall see clearly the whole way by which He has led me, when I shall know fully the spring and ocean of that love which is from everlasting to everlasting, when my dark mind shall grasp the whole plan of the universe, by which every atom, and every being, saved or lost, is brought to yield eternal glory to God and the Lamb, then I shall understand the word that is written, "Salvation belongeth unto the Lord", and I shall be enabled to join the new song of the innumerable company before the throne, "Salvation to our God, which sitteth upon the throne, and unto the Lamb" (Revelation 7:10).

In what remains we have a description of the stream of grace which flows from this Fountain of living waters. A twofold stream is here set before us, the one part reconciliation to Himself, the other the gift of the ministry. They are mentioned together in like manner: "We have received grace and apostleship" (Romans 1:5). These two gifts are not inseparable. Many have been reconciled to God who have not got the ministry committed to them. Women, for example, are made partakers of *grace,* but never of *apostleship;* for Paul says, "I suffer not a woman to teach, nor to usurp authority over the man, but to be in silence" (1 Timothy 2:12). Those also who are converted in mature years, when they are deeply engaged in some profession, do not seem to be called upon to change their business, and undertake the work of the ministry, unless in extraordinary times, and by a very clear call from heaven: "Let every man abide in the same calling wherein he was called" (1 Corinthians 7:20).

When these two, grace and apostleship, are united in one man, O! what a gift is this from the God of all grace. What amazing love it is not only to save our guilty souls, but to make us instrumentally the saviours of the souls of others: "According to thy manifold mercies, thou gavest them saviours, who saved them out of the hand of their enemies" (Nehemiah 9:27). It is Christ alone who gives faithful pastors, and from Him they should be

70

sought. This is one of the gifts which He obtained by dying for sinners, "He gave some apostles, and some prophets, and some evangelists, and some pastors, and teachers, for the perfecting of the saints, for the work of the ministry, for the edifying of the body of Christ" (Ephesians 4:11). It is Christ alone who guides ministers to the sphere where He wishes them to shine. Happy the pastor who allows no hand but Christ's to place or to remove him. It is Christ alone who gives them all their light and brightness, all their gifts and graces, the gifts of prayer, eloquence, knowledge; the graces of faith, love, zeal, perseverance, boldness. All this was taught to John in the island of Patmos, when he saw "one like the Son of man walking in the midst of the seven golden candlesticks, and he had in his right hand seven stars" (Revelation 1:13, 16). It is Christ alone who gives ministers all their success: "I have planted, Apollos watered; but God gave the increase" (1 Corinthians 3:6). He can take away the blessing from a slothful, self-pleasing, self-conceited minister. He can bless one who is weak in body, weak in argument, weak in everything. When I glance for a moment at the weight, vastness, responsibility, blessedness, and glory of this work, these words rise up before me: "Unto me who am less than the least of all saints, is this grace given, that I should preach among the Gentiles the unsearchable riches of Christ." When I consider the urgent need of unconverted men, the shortness of the time, the awfulness of eternity, and the mercy that has come to my own soul, I am forced to cry, "Necessity is laid upon me; yea, woe is unto me, if I preach not the gospel" (1 Corinthians 9:16).

# 26.    God in Christ
Reconciling the World

*To wit, that God was in Christ,*
*reconciling the world unto himself, not imputing*
*their trespasses unto them; and hath committed unto us the*
*word of reconciliation.*

2 CORINTHIANS 5:19

IN THESE WORDS we have an epitome, or short description of the gospel ministry.

1. *Observe the manner in which God approaches sinners in the gospel:* "God was in Christ." If God had come to us without a Mediator, it would have been to destroy. In His unchangeable nature He is holy, sin-repelling, and sin-consuming. This is the glory of God, His moral image, without which He could not be Jehovah. As surely as fire devours wood by its physical nature, so surely God must destroy sinners by His glorious moral nature. Therefore it is written, "Upon the wicked he shall rain snares, fire, and brimstone, and an horrible tempest; this shall be the portion of their cup; *for* the righteous Lord loveth righteousness" (Psalm 11:6-7). And again, "Thou art of purer eyes than to behold evil, and canst not look on iniquity" (Habakkuk 1:13). And "we know him that hath said, Vengeance *belongeth* unto me, I will recompense, saith the Lord. And again, the Lord shall judge his people. It is a fearful thing to fall into the hands of the living God. For our God is a consuming fire" (Hebrews 10:30-31; 12:29). If God had drawn near to us without His justice being satisfied in the blood and obedience of the Lord Jesus, His justice must have broken out upon us, and sought its satisfaction in our everlasting punishment. Glory to God in the highest, that God did not come to us without Christ, that He did not come upon us naked, guilty, defenceless, without a shelter for our heavy laden soul. He put the Mediator between Him and us: "For there is one God, and one Mediator between God and men, the man Christ Jesus, who gave himself a ransom for all" (1 Timothy 2:5-6). "God was in Christ." Christ is the meeting place of a holy God, and hell-deserving sinners: "Having therefore boldness to enter into the holiest by the blood of Jesus, let us draw near." When the high priest

72

entered within the vail, on the day of atonement, he carried with him a basin filled with the blood of a bullock, slain as an atonement for himself and his house. He dipped his finger in the blood and sprinkled it upon the mercy-seat, and before the mercy-seat seven times. He then carried in another basin filled with the blood of a goat, slain for the sins of the people. Dipping his finger into the blood he sprinkled it upon the mercy-seat, and before the mercy-seat. The mercy-seat was of pure gold, the floor was covered with gold, yet he did not fear lest he should soil it. The mercy-seat and the golden pavement were wetted with blood. His feet stood upon the blood. That blood represented the blood of Christ. And the high priest standing on the sprinkled blood represented the only way in which a sinner can come to a holy Jehovah. God meets us in Christ. O sinner! hast thou come to God in Christ, hast thou entered into the holiest by the blood of Jesus. If not, thou art yet unpardoned, and ready to perish. Some have very weak notions of conversion. They seem to think that to weep at a sermon, to pray with a glow of feeling, to amend the life a little, is true conversion — whereas it is turning to God in Christ: "Ye turned to God from idols" (1 Thessalonians 1:9). Except thou be thus converted, thou wilt never see the kingdom of God.

2. *Observe the extent of the gospel remedy:* "Reconciling the world unto himself." There can be no doubt that the whole world will not be saved: "Strait is the gate, and narrow is the way that leadeth unto life, and few there be that find it." The awful transactions of the judgment-day are summed up in these solemn words: "These shall go away into everlasting punishment, but the righteous into life eternal" (Matthew 25:46). One amazing portion of the human race will depart speechless, conscience-stricken, self-condemned, into a hell as everlasting as the heaven of those who are saved. O self-deceived Universalist! it is the same word which describes the eternity of heaven and the eternity of hell. There can be no doubt that God has chosen a peculiar people out of this world: "Blessed is the man whom thou choosest, and causest to approach unto thee" (Psalm 65:4). Six times over, in the seventeenth chapter of John, does Jesus call them "the men which thou gavest me", and He says, "I pray for them, I pray not for the world". And yet it is equally true that "God will have all men to be saved, and to come unto the knowledge of the truth" (1 Timothy 2:4). He is "Long-suffering to us-ward, not willing that any should perish, but that all should come to repentance" (2 Peter 3:9). "God was in Christ, reconciling *the world* to himself." The gospel is truly and sincerely addressed "to every creature under heaven". The calls and invitations of God to wicked men are not mere words

73

of course, far less are they deceitful and lying words; they are true as God is true. There is not even the shadow of falsehood in them. Hear the words of a master in Israel: "There is all in God that is good, and perfect, and excellent, in our desires and wishes for the conversion and salvation of wicked men. As for instance, there is a love to holiness absolutely considered, or an agree-ableness of holiness to His nature and will; or in other words, to His natural inclination. The holiness and happiness of the creature, absolutely considered, are things that He loves. These things are infinitely more agreeable to His nature than to ours. There is all in God that belongs to our desire of the holiness and happiness of unconverted men and reprobates, excepting what implies imperfection. All that is consistent with infinite knowledge, wisdom, power, self-sufficience, infinite happiness, and immutability. Therefore there is no reason that His absolute prescience, or His wise deter-mination and ordering what is future, should hinder His expressing this disposition of His nature, in like manner as we are wont to express such a disposition in ourselves, viz., by calls, and invitations, and the like." O sinner! it is true that God has no pleasure in your dying, but had rather that you would turn from your wicked ways and live. God honestly, sincerely, and with all His heart, beseeches you to be reconciled through the blood of Jesus. He is willing this day to cover you with the blood and obedience of the Lord Jesus, so that He may consistently, with His just and holy nature, not impute your trespasses unto you. Why has He spared you out of hell to this day? Only because "he is not willing that you should perish". Why has He followed you with personal and family mercies, comforts, deliverances? "The goodness of God leadeth thee to repentance" (Romans 2:4). Why has He sent frowns of providence upon you, poverty, sickness, bereavements, disappointments, like wave upon wave? Is not this the answer: "Whom I love, I rebuke and chasten; be zealous therefore, and repent" (Revelation 3:19). Why has the Spirit striven with you in the Bible, through ministers, and in secret prayer? Is it not that the holy loving Spirit desires you to turn to Christ, and is "vexed", and "grieved", and "quenched", by your "always resisting?" (Acts 7:51). Why, above all, does Christ offer Himself freely to every creature, why has He knocked at your door, and stretched out His hands to you all day long? Ah! read here the answer, which you will remem-ber to your everlasting agony in hell, if you turn not, "How often would I have gathered your children together, even as a hen gathereth her chickens under her wings, and ye would not!" (Matthew 23:37). O sinner! the Lord Jesus Christ is like the manna. It fell round about the tents of Israel every morning, so that no Israelite could go out of his tent without either gathering it, or trampling it below his feet. So the Lord Jesus is laid down at thy feet. Thou must either take Him as thy Surety, thy Saviour, thy Lord, or trample Him below thy feet.

# 27.  Ambassadors for Christ

*Now then we are ambassadors for Christ,*
*as though God did beseech you by us: we pray you in Christ's stead,*
*be ye reconciled to God.*

2 CORINTHIANS 5:20

1. *MEDITATE ON THE GROUND of the gospel message,* verse 21. "He hath made him to be sin", etc. What a remarkable description of Christ is here given, "He knew no sin". He was pure in His birth. The angel that came to Mary called Him "that holy thing which shall be born of thee". He was pure in His life, "He did no sin, neither was guile found his his mouth" (1 Peter 2:22). He was pure in His death, "He offered himself without spot unto God". But here we are told "he knew no sin". He did not know the feeling of sin. He did not know the swelling of pride, the burning of lust, the rankling of envy in His pure bosom. He knew suffering well, but He knew no sin. Learn, O my soul, the loveliness of Christ. "He is altogether lovely." His loveliness consists mainly in this, that He knew no sin. It is this that ravishes the hearts of the redeemed above while they sing, "Who shall not fear thee, and glorify thy name, for thou only art holy". Learn the suitableness of Christ. If Christ had had a spot of sin He could not have suffered for ours. "Such an High Priest became us who is holy, harmless, undefiled, and separate from sinners.

But how did God deal with this sinless One? "He hath made him to be sin for us." In Isaiah 53:6 we are told, "The Lord laid on him the iniquities of us all". But here it is described in a more dreadful manner. The Lord heaped upon Him the thousands and millions of our sins, till at last He was so covered, in God's sight, that nothing but sin appeared. He was looked upon, by His Father, as one entire mass of sin. He was dealt with by God as if He were all sin from the sole of the foot to the crown of the head. Learn, O my soul, the deep agonies of Christ; He knew no sin, and yet He was made sin. Nothing can be more agonising to a pure mind, than to have sins imputed to him. This was Christ's deepest sorrow. Hence the heart-rending cries recorded in the 22nd, 40th and 69th Psalms; cries that often resounded through the silent vale of Kedron. Learn the amazing love of Christ; "it passeth knowledge".

But why was He made sin? It was "that we might be made the righteousness of God in him". Just as Christ was so covered with our innumerable sins that in the eye of a holy God He appeared one mass of sin, so the vilest of sinners who consents to be found in Christ, is so covered with His glorious righteousness, that in the eye of God he appears one mass of divine righteousness. The sinner is lost and swallowed up in the righteousness of Christ.

O my sinful soul! what an amazing provision is here set before thee for thy complete pardon and acceptance with God. As truly as Christ was made the sin of men, so truly may I be made the righteousness of God. As truly as our sin covered Him, so that none of His heavenly beauty appeared, so truly may His righteousness cover me that none of my hellish blackness may appear. Christ held down His head for shame on account of my sin, I may hold up my head in peace on account of His righteousness.

2. *Meditate on the gospel embassy,* verse 20: "We are," etc. Christ was God's greatest ambassador. He was "the messenger of the covenant". He was sent to bind up the broken-hearted, to proclaim liberty to the captives, and the opening of the prison to them that are bound." He was "the faithful Witness". He was sent to tell men the way to the Father. But when He ascended up on on high He sent His believing followers in His name, "Peace be unto you; as my Father hath sent me, even so send I you" (John 20:21). "When He ascended up on high, he gave some apostles, and some prophets, and some evangelists, and some pastors, and teachers, for the perfecting of the saints, for the work of the ministry, for the edifying of the body of Christ." "Now then (all faithful ministers may say) we are ambassadors for Christ."

(i) This shows that ministers should speak with authority. The people were astonished at the doctrine of Christ, "for he taught them as one having authority, and not as the scribes". He spoke with a holy certainty and boldness, and so should ministers now. "These things command and teach; let no man despise thy youth" (1 Timothy 4:11-12). A faithful minister should be like Jeremiah (1:18), "I have made thee this day a defenced city, and an iron pillar, and brazen walls against the whole land". He should hear God saying to him as He did to Ezekiel (2:7), "Thou shalt speak my words unto them, whether they will hear, or whether they will forbear". How fearful is the curse threatened if we alter the gospel of Christ, Galatians 1:8; if we add to, or take away from, the message committed unto us, Revelation 22:18-19.

(ii) Ministers should speak with divine tenderness. "God is love", and so should His ambassadors be. There is in the heart of God the deepest compassion for perishing sinners. Hear His words (Deuteronomy 5:29), "O that there were such an heart in them, that they would fear me, and keep all my commandments always, that it might be well with them, and with their children for ever" (compare 32:29; Ezekiel 33:11). When God was manifest in flesh He showed this holy tenderness through His whole life (Luke 19:41), "When he was come near, he beheld the city, and wept over it" (compare Matthew 23:37). Such should be the heart of every faithful minister. Paul used to preach with many tears, Acts 20:31. His tears often fell upon the parchment on which he wrote his epistles, Philippians 3:18; 2 Corinthians 2:4.

Surely if we could realize an eternal hell into which the most are dropping, an eternal heaven which the most are losing, and a divine Saviour whom the most are rejecting, we would preach as Jeremiah did, "O that my head were waters, and mine eyes a fountain of tears" (9:1). We would be mercifully bold, like the angels at Sodom, laying hands on lingering sinners, and pulling them out of the fire.

(iii) This shows the message which ministers bear. "We pray you in Christ's stead, be ye reconciled unto God." There is a quarrel between sinners and a holy God. "God is angry with the wicked every day." The dark heavy clouds of divine anger are resting upon their heads, ready to break every moment. Sinners are angry at God. Their carnal mind is enmity against God. They are night and day fighting against God. Now God sends His ministers with a white flag of truce, and He puts this word in their mouths, "Be ye reconciled unto God". O my soul, hast thou heard and received the "good tidings of great joy"? Have I submitted to the way of pardon here revealed? Then in a moment God's anger is all turned away, and my heart is changed from bitter enmity to love and praise.

# 28. Earnest Heed to the Message

*Therefore we ought to give the more
earnest heed to the things which we have heard, lest at any time
we should let them slip.*

HEBREWS 2:1

COULD WE LOOK into the secret history of believers, what woeful declensions might be pointed out. How many, who began the conflict well, have fallen under the blows of Apollyon. How many are there of whom God complains: "What iniquity have ye found in me that ye are gone far from me" (Jeremiah 2:5). How many of whom Jesus complains, "I have this against thee, that thou hast left thy first love" (Revelation 2:4). The spring of all these sad declensions is to be found in "letting slip the things which we have heard".

1. *Meditate on the times when Christians are in danger of letting the gospel slip.*

(i) *A time of worldly prosperity.* An old divine says, "Quails often make a lean soul". "He gave them their request, but sent leanness into their souls." When a man is under conviction of sin, divine things often absorb every other anxiety. That text is ever before him, "What shall it profit a man to gain the whole world, and lose his own soul?". He becomes careless of his person, for he feels that he would be decking a body condemned to the burning. He becomes careless of his business, for the matter of his forgiveness is unsettled. He walks among the things of time, looking through them into the things of eternity. What a vain shadow is this world to an awakened soul. O! how that soul sickens at the vain companies of an unbelieving world; how he loathes their dances and wanton songs. But when that soul has found true rest in Christ, sometimes the world begins to smile again. He begins to launch out into business, or a more lucrative situation is offered to him. His attention is a little diverted from eternal things; he becomes more keen about the things of time. He begins to lose his fresh hold of Christ. He is letting slip the things which he heard. So it was with Lot. When he first came from Haran he left all for God. He followed Abraham, a simple shepherd lad with staff in hand. But when he got flocks, and herds, and tents, and when he saw

78

the plain of Sodom well watered everywhere, he went and pitched his tent toward Sodom, Genesis 13. So it was with Demas. At one time he seemed to leave all for Christ. He became the companion of self-denying Paul. But soon his eye was caught with the glitter of gold. He lets slip the things which he heard. He bids farewell to the believer's joys and trials: "Demas hath forsaken me, having loved this present world" (2 Timothy 4:10). O my soul, "love not the world, neither the things that are in the world. If any man love the world, the love of the Father is not in him".

(ii) *A time of persecution.* "For every ten bodies which persecution has killed, it has slain a thousand souls." We are told of the seed that sprung up so quickly in stony places, that "when the sun was up it withered away", and Jesus explains this of those who, "when tribulation or persecution ariseth because of the word, by and by they are offended" (Matthew 13:21). Some people are brought to Christ with little or no persecution. They attain "to joy and peace in believing", no man forbidding them. They begin to think that the offence of the cross has ceased, and that the solemn warnings of tribulation to the believer were intended for a bye-gone generation. Suddenly their sky is overcast. They begin to be hated, and buffeted, and opposed for their attachment to Christ. An awful prospect is before them. Either they must breast the tide of scorn and reproach that is now flowing in upon them, perhaps from their dearest friends, or else they must let slip the things which they have heard. Ah! how often, in such an hour, the soul shrinks back from an open confession of Christ before men, refuses to bear the cross, and falls into unholy compromise with an unbelieving world. Storms try the vessel, and persecution tries the believer. When Peter was in peace he could say, "Though all men forsake thee, yet will not I". But when the hour of trial came, he said with oaths and curses, "I know not the man".

2. *Meditate on the remedy.* "We ought to give the more earnest heed," etc.

(i) *Increase thy diligence in the means of grace.* If you have truly found the Lord Jesus, be often at the spot where you have met with Him. Every true disciple should often resort to Gethsemane, John 18:2. If you have found Him in the Word, be faithful and diligent in meeting Him there. If you begin to let your Bible slip, you are beginning to let Jesus slip. If you found Him in secret prayer, give the more earnest heed to meet Him often there. It is a sweet trysting-place with Jesus, "within the vail". If you let slip the throne of grace, you let Him slip who sits thereon. Have you found Jesus in the sanctuary, then "love the habitation of his house, and the place where his honour dwelleth" (Psalm 26:8). Has He revealed Himself to you in the breaking of

79

bread, then "continue stedfastly in the apostles' doctrine, and in fellowship, and in breaking of bread, and in prayer" (Acts 2:42).

(ii) *Feed on Christ in the ordinances.* Many love the ordinances who love not Christ. Many are occupied about the shell who never taste the kernel of the gospel. These are Sardians who "have a name to live while they are dead". These are talkers about the gospel and its ministers; but "the talk of their lips tendeth to penury". If you have found Christ in ordinances, give earnest heed to find Him more and more. Penetrate through every vail to the living Saviour, and the living God. Do not rest in a form of prayer if you find not Christ. "Bodily service profiteth little". O my soul, abhor the cloak of formality. It is an abomination to God and man. "It is iniquity, even the solemn meeting." But O how sweet are ordinances when we can say, "He brought me into his banqueting house, and his banner over me was love.

(iii) *Watch against occasions of letting slip.* If you knew the deceitfulness, the desperate and unsearchable wickedness of your own heart, and if you knew the adversary who accuses you day and night, you would be sober and vigilant. Watch your own heart, its infirmities and tendencies; "Keep thy heart above all keeping, for out of it are the issues of life" (Proverbs 4:23). Watch the roaring lion; be not ignorant of his devices, 1 Peter 5:8. Watch the world, for you are in an enemy's country, "The whole world lieth in wickedness" (1 John 5:19). Above all, keep your eye on Jesus. You cannot hold Him if He does not hold you. "Cast all your care upon him, for he careth for you" (1 Peter 5:7).